How to Help Your Child with

Homework

How to Help
Your Child with
Homework

The Complete Guide to Encouraging Good
Study Habits and Ending the Homework Wars
(updated and revised edition)

**For Parents
of Children
Ages 6–13**

Jeanne Shay Schumm, Ph.D.

free spirit
PUBLiSHiNG®

Helping kids
help themselves™
since 1983

Library of Congress Cataloging-in-Publication Data

Schumm, Jeanne Shay, 1947–
    How to help your child with homework : the complete guide to encouraging good study habits and ending the homework wars : for parents of children ages 6/13 / Jeanne Shay Schumm.—Rev. and updated ed.
        p. cm.
    Previous ed. entered under Radencich, Marguerite C.
    Includes index.
    ISBN 1-57542-168-2
1. Homework—United States. 2. Education—Parent participation—United States. I. Title.
    LB1048.S35 2005
    372.13'0281—dc22   200402436

J/Parent Teacher

At the time of this book's publication, all facts and figures cited are the most current available; all telephone numbers, addresses, and Web site URLs are accurate and active; all publications, organizations, Web sites, and other resources exist as described in this book; and all have been verified as of October 2004. The author and Free Spirit Publishing make no warranty or guarantee concerning the information and materials given out by organizations or content found at Web sites, and we are not responsible for any changes that occur after this book's publication. If you find an error or believe that a resource listed here is not as described, please contact Free Spirit Publishing. Parents, teachers, and other adults: We strongly urge you to monitor children's use of the Internet.

Thanks to Dr. Arlene Brett, my colleague at the University of Miami, for reviewing Chapter 9.

Edited by Pamela Espeland and Catherine Broberg
Book Design by Percolator
Index by Pamela Van Huss

10 9 8 7 6 5 4 3 2 1
Printed in the United States of America

Free Spirit Publishing Inc.
217 Fifth Avenue North, Suite 200
Minneapolis, MN 55401-1299
(612) 338-2068
help4kids@freespirit.com
www.freespirit.com

To Jack,

You are my sunshine.

Love, Oma

Contents

List of Reproducible Pages

Preface

Fifteen years have passed since Margie Radencich and I first wrote *How to Help Your Child with Homework*. We wrote the book because as teachers and tutors, we were often asked by our friends, relatives, neighbors, and the parents of our students for advice on handling the homework issue. Our ideas for the first edition came from our own research, our reading of the research of others, and conversations with parents about what they had tried and what had been successful for them. At the time I was also the parent of a 14-year-old daughter, Jamie, who helped me gain personal experience as a homework helper.

A great deal has changed since this book was originally published. First, as research has continued to underscore the importance of parents being involved in their children's academic lives, the role of parents in education has received widespread attention. When this book first came out, few books provided parents with specific strategies for facilitating home learning. Today, much is written about the role of parents in the educational progress of their children.

Second, the nature of reading instruction in schools has evolved—today, there is more emphasis on early reading, word recognition, and reading comprehension. Third, technology in the home has matured.

Computers are now widely available and are becoming less expensive. The amount of information available to students for homework assistance is mind-boggling. Things have changed.

This new edition draws on my research over the years, particularly in the field of reading. My daughter, Jamie, has also contributed to this book in a new way. She is now a kindergarten teacher and lends me advice from her own work with parents and their children. Moreover, Jamie is now the mother of a 4-year-old son, Jack, and watching his home learning experiences is probably the best experience of my life.

A final thing has changed since the last revision of *How to Help Your Child with Homework*. I am doing the revisions by myself, as Margie Radencich passed away in 1998. Margie and I attended the University of Miami as doctoral students together. She later became director of Reading and Language Arts for Miami-Dade County Public Schools, a professor at University of South Florida, and President of the Florida Reading Association. Margie's legacy of caring about providing successful learning opportunities for all children lives on.

Jeanne Shay Schumm, Ph.D.

Introduction

"I didn't do my homework because you forgot to remind me."

"I didn't do my homework because my parents came home late from work."

"I did my homework but the hard drive crashed."

"I did my homework but I left it on the bus."

"I did my homework but it was stolen from my locker."

"I did my homework but my baby sister wrecked it."

"I did my homework but the dog ate it."

"I left my homework in my pocket and my mom put my jeans in the wash."

Teachers have heard excuses like these since the first teacher made the first homework assignment. As long as teachers keep giving homework, most students will keep trying to get out of doing it.

Why do teachers bother with homework? Why do they continue to inflict homework on kids, their parents, and themselves? In fact, there are several excellent reasons:

- Homework encourages children to practice skills they haven't yet fully learned.

- Homework gives children opportunities to review skills they might otherwise forget.

- Homework enriches and broadens a child's knowledge.

- Homework teaches responsibility.

- Homework allows for tasks that are too time-consuming to be finished during school hours.

As a parent, you can probably think of a few more reasons. You may remember times from your own childhood when a homework assignment made the difference between fully understanding a subject and barely grasping it, between excelling on a test and just scraping by. There may have been occasions when you actually *enjoyed* doing your homework—when you sat at the kitchen table or sprawled on the living room floor, working at your own pace on a project that fascinated you, without the distractions of the classroom.

Of course, this is not your homework we're talking about here, but your child's. You have taken on a new role, that of a homework helper. This role is one that can be confusing and frustrating. You probably truly want to help your child with this daily task—and know you need to help—but you may not know how to get started. This book can help you take those first steps. It will outline how to create a homework plan, set up a study area, deal with numerous problems that may occur, and help you instill a love of learning in your child.

By deciding to help your child with homework, you will start paving the road to success for your child—in school and beyond.

"Once children learn how to learn, nothing is going to narrow their mind. The essence of teaching is to make learning contagious, to have one idea spark another."

MARVA COLLINS

Getting Started

The two-way street between home and school

Here's what happens when parents are informed and active in their children's academic lives: students are more motivated and experience more success; parents connect with their children in new ways; and teachers and schools develop a collaborative relationship with parents. In short, everyone wins. Parental involvement, in fact, is encouraged by the National PTA *(www.pta.org)** and teacher professional groups such as the International Reading Association *(www.reading.org)* and the National Council of Teachers of Mathematics *(www.nctm.org)*.

It goes without saying that the better your relationship is with your child's teacher and school, the more positive your child's school experience will be. Because homework is part of your child's school experience, it's wise to make that relationship a two-way street. Following are some suggestions for accomplishing this.

Talk to your child about school.

Ask your child to tell you about what happens during the day. What does your child like best about school? What does she like least about it?** The more you know, the more prepared you'll be if problems arise.

---

*This book lists several Web sites. The World Wide Web is enormous and fluid; please be aware that sites come and go and URLs (Internet addresses) change, so the information listed here may not always be current and accurate. But it should give you a start in the right direction. When in doubt, use a search engine.

**For ease of reading, the sections of this book alternate in the use of male and female pronouns.

Plan to meet with your child's teacher at least three times during the school year.

Communicate your willingness to cooperate with the teacher. Don't wait for a personal invitation; an open house (most schools hold them annually) is an excellent opportunity to have a brief conversation. If you need more time, make an appointment.

Learn about the homework policy for the school district, school, and class.

Some school districts have *homework policies* that schools and individual teachers are required to follow. Such policies determine how much homework students should receive. In other districts, individual schools and/or teachers are responsible for setting their own homework policies. Find out about the policies that affect your child. Ask how often homework is assigned, when it is assigned, and how homework will affect your child's grade. Also, learn about what support for homework is available through Web sites sponsored by your district, school, and/or classroom teacher.

Learn about your child's teacher.

Dr. Linda Blanton, an expert in special education, recommends that parents take time at the beginning of the school year to learn about their child's teacher.* She suggests finding out if the teacher is certified and areas of certification. With current teacher shortages, many teachers are teaching out of their field. Parents should be informed

about this. Find out how long your child's teacher has been teaching and whether he or she graduated from an accredited teacher education institution. The National Council for the Accreditation of Teacher Education is the most prestigious of these accreditation organizations. Your child's principal can provide this information.

Learn about the curriculum at your child's school.

What is your child being taught? How is she being taught? Many schools provide parents with written summaries of the curriculum. In other schools, teachers describe the curriculum during parent meetings or open houses. Ask whether this information is provided as a matter of course; if it isn't, tell the teacher you'd appreciate having it. Learn about what your child is learning.

Find out how you will be informed about your child's progress.

Will children bring papers home on a weekly basis? What dates are report cards issued? Will you receive updates between report cards? Does your school have an online gradebook with parental access?

Act quickly if you suspect that a problem exists.

Tell the teacher that you want to meet, and make an appointment as soon as possible. Don't just show up unannounced! Spur-of-the-moment conferences translate into incomplete information. They aren't fair to you, the teacher, or your child.

Sometimes a teacher will notice a problem before the parents do. Typically, a teacher will initiate communication by

---

*Linda Blanton, "Questions to Ask the Teacher About Your Child's Education," *Miami Herald,* August 10, 2003; National Council for Accreditation of Teacher Education, *www.ncate.org/newsbrfs/blanton.htm* (accessed October 5, 2004).

sending a note home with the child or emailing you. Be sure to respond, either with a phone call or with a note of your own. Depending on the nature of the problem, you may want to schedule a conference to discuss it.

If your child is having difficulties doing schoolwork, make sure there are no hidden physical causes. A visit to your pediatrician, ophthalmologist, or audiologist can uncover any that might exist.

How much homework is enough?

How can you tell if your child is getting the right amount of homework? First, it helps to understand that homework policies differ widely from state to state, school to school, and teacher to teacher. Typically, the amount of homework increases as the child moves up to higher grades.

- If your child consistently tells you that he has no homework or has "done it on the bus," check with the teacher. If what your child is saying is true, the teacher might be willing to assign more challenging homework or suggest other home learning activities.

- If your child's homework load allows no time for play, check with the teacher. The homework load might be excessive. Discuss this possibility with the teacher and try to work out a solution together.

Between these two extremes, it's sometimes difficult to figure out what is an appropriate amount of homework. Some

children take longer than others to complete assignments; also, the homework load may be heavier or lighter at certain times of the year. A general guideline for daily homework is 10 minutes per grade. Using that template, fourth graders would get 40 minutes worth of homework and eighth graders 80 minutes. Some educators recommend more homework, while others feel that the school day is long enough and any amount of homework is too much. If you are in total disagreement with the policy followed by your child's teacher or school, schedule a conference and try to reach a compromise.

How can you tell if the content of your child's homework is appropriate? Here's a good rule of thumb: *Homework should not involve anything that is brand new to the child.* If your child consistently requires a lot of help with homework, schedule a conference with the teacher. Possible problems may include:

- Your child may not be paying attention in class.

- Your child may have a listening or memory problem and may not be learning what is taught in class.

- Your child may have a learning difference that is getting in the way of his understanding of the assignment. (For more information on learning differences, see page 22.)

- Your child may be using homework as a way to get your attention.

- Your child's teacher may be assigning work that has not yet been taught in class.

- The assignments may be unclear, unfair, or without purpose.

Once you identify the problem, you and the teacher can work together toward a solution. Keep in mind that most teachers really *want* to help their students. If you maintain a positive attitude, most problems can be solved at the classroom level.

Help!

? **"My daughter will start first grade soon and I've heard she'll be getting homework regularly. I'd like to get off to a good start with this and set the tone for years to come, but this is all new to me, too. How do I create the right 'working relationship' with my daughter?"**

Hold a family meeting to discuss homework and to have a general "pep" session about the possibilities of home learning. Plan a scheduled homework time and plan and organize the study center (see pages 11–12 for more ideas on this). Talk about roles and responsibilities. Most important, set a positive tone and be prepared to provide support and encouragement.

? **"My son's teacher requires him to do homework, but she never grades it. For example, every week he has to look up 15 words in a dictionary and copy the definitions. But as far as I can tell, the teacher just puts a check in her grade book that my son did the homework, but doesn't grade it at all. Is this sound educational practice?"**

Research indicates that homework is most effective when teachers grade it and give students feedback about it. If homework is just busywork, it serves no real purpose.

Talk to your son's teacher. Perhaps she reviews homework with the students in class. Or maybe she doesn't grade specific assignments but monitors her students' performance on homework in another way. If neither seems to be the case in your son's class, ask the teacher how your son (and you) can get more feedback on the work he does at home.

? **"My daughter usually understands her homework, but she works through it too quickly and makes a lot of mistakes."**

Check your daughter's homework after she completes it and have her make the necessary corrections. Limit your help to general suggestions for improvement. (*Examples:* "You've forgotten two periods in this paragraph. Find where they belong." Or "Five of your math problems seem to be wrong. Check your answers.") Another alternative is to block off a specific amount of time each day as a homework period. If your daughter finishes her homework before the end of the period, let her spend the rest of the time on schoolwork-related activities you give to her. If she doesn't finish her homework in the allotted time, make an assessment of what is left to be done and how well she used her time; then make a decision to go forward or to stop. Finally, you might consider starting a "reward system" for neat and accurate work.

? **"My son is in the fifth grade. His school decided to 'departmentalize' this year. In other words, he now has different teachers for math, language arts, science, and social studies. The idea**

behind this change is to help get the children ready for middle school, but from my point of view, it's a disaster! My son can't keep track of his homework assignments from class to class, and he never seems to know when he's going to have a test. All of this switching around is very confusing to him—and to me!"

Set up a meeting with your son's teachers right away—don't delay. Request that all four teachers be present (perhaps you can schedule a meeting on a teacher planning day). Explain the situation and suggest that you all put your heads together on an action plan. Work with the teachers to develop a system for monitoring the plan and making certain that your son is keeping up with homework and is prepared for tests. (Perhaps your son can keep one assignment sheet for all classes; see pages 144 and 145 for examples you can copy and use.) Once you decide on a plan with the teachers, let your son know what it is. Be patient; it may take some time before the plan becomes routine and all of the bugs are worked out.

"If I have questions about home-work, can't I just email my daughter's teacher?"

Like most people, individual teachers have different opinions about email. Some teachers are online constantly and like frequent email communication with parents. Others rarely check their email. Obviously, it takes time to respond to each parent's emails, which reduces the time teachers have for lesson planning. Ask your daughter's teacher about email preferences. If the teacher encourages email communication, use the following guidelines:

- Reserve emails for essentials—be prudent.

- Write messages that are direct and short—be concise.

- Don't write anything you wouldn't say to the teacher's face—be respectful.

- If the teacher doesn't respond, call or make an appointment to see the teacher—be flexible.

Who should help with homework?

Many parents feel they don't have the skills to help their children with homework. Yet, research has shown that the quality of the parent-child interaction is more important than the actual techniques used. You might be surprised at what a good teacher you can be!

Helping with homework, however, doesn't have to be your responsibility alone. You may discover that more than one family member is willing and able to lend a hand. As you decide who should help your child with homework, consider these questions:

- Is there someone in your family who's a "natural teacher"? Maybe it's a parent. Or maybe it's a sibling or other relative who lives nearby and is willing to help.

- Is there someone in your family who's especially knowledgeable about or talented in a particular subject area? Maybe Dad studied French in college. Maybe big sister is a math whiz.

You might also look beyond your immediate family. If your child spends the after-school hours with a sitter, perhaps the sitter can help. Or maybe the sitter you regularly call for weekday or weekend evenings can lend a hand. And don't forget about other children your child knows. Kids who study with friends can help each other. For the sake of simplicity, this book is written to the parent and assumes that the parent is the one who will most likely be involved. But that doesn't have to be the case. Ask around and you may find that help is available from other sources.

Of course, you should exercise good judgment in any of these arrangements. Be certain the person really wants to help and understands this basic principle: *Homework should never be done for the child.* Also make sure that the person has the time. Helping with homework should not put an excessive burden on anyone, particularly siblings. If big brother has an especially busy school and social schedule, the added responsibility may not be beneficial to him or to the child in need of assistance.

You should also be aware that online help may be available to your child. Some schools and school districts have Web sites with online "Dial-a-Teacher" support. Such sites typically include links, frequently asked questions, and email responses for individual queries. See Chapter 9 to learn more about online help.

Why and how to set a homework schedule

Children (and adults) respond well to structure and consistency. We all feel more secure when we know what to expect. (If you need convincing, think back to how you felt on your child's first day of kindergarten, compared to how you feel now when your child leaves for school.) This sense of security is the main reason for setting a firm schedule for homework sessions. Another good reason is that this eliminates one of the most common battles in the Homework Wars: arguing about when to do it. Finally, setting a schedule ensures that homework will get done by a reasonable hour. Many children are natural procrastinators; if we let them, they'll put off starting their homework (or any other chore) until the last possible minute—or they won't do it at all.

You may be blessed with a child who does her homework without prodding or reminding. If so, she should be allowed to set her own schedule, with only occasional monitoring from you. However, it's far more likely that you will need to get directly involved in this process. In deciding when your child's homework sessions should be scheduled, keep these guidelines in mind:

- Most kids need some time to unwind after school and before settling in to do their homework—but they shouldn't wait until it's so late that they're too tired to work through it effectively.

- Children have trouble concentrating when they're hungry. If homework must be done before dinner, offer a healthy snack. (Please, no sugary snacks or caffeinated soft drinks.)

- Younger children have a harder time sitting still for extended periods than older children. Fortunately, short study sessions often lead to more learning than longer ones. For example, it's better to practice flash cards for two 10-minute sessions than one 20-minute marathon.

Most families already have their own schedules—times when people arrive home from school and work, times when they sit down to dinner, times when the kids go to sports or lessons. Although it will almost certainly be a challenge, try to fit homework in when it will be least disruptive. On the other hand, homework should be a priority, and it should be taken seriously. There is no one best place to fit it in because each family's situation is different. Rest assured, however, that once you set a schedule and stick to it, it *does* get easier. And once your child gets used to the idea that homework will be done no matter what, you can afford to be flexible when the need arises.

Homework Schedule

PREPARED FOR: Luis   PREPARED BY: m♡m (xoxo)

4:00-4:30	After school play time.
4:30-5:30	Start homework. FIRST, figure out what you need to do. NEXT, decide which things you want me to help you with. (Do HARDEST homework first!)
5:30-6:00	Stop homework. Play time.
6:00-7:00	Dinner.
7:00-7:30	Finish any leftover homework.
7:30-8:30	Play or TV time (IF HOMEWORK IS DONE). Check with me BEFORE turning on the TV!
8:30	Bedtime.

There is one issue that may need addressing in advance: the problem of the Overprogrammed Child. Parents naturally want their children to have everything. However, the child who has piano lessons on Mondays, karate lessons on Tuesdays and Thursdays, and scouts on Wednesdays may be doing too much. Kids need time for homework and chores, and they also need free time for play. If your child is involved in a variety of activities, you may want to reassess the situation—especially if her grades are suffering or there are signs of emerging emotional difficulties. A few signs to watch for include:

- refusing to go to school or talk about school

- refusing to do homework

- physical ailments with no identifiable medical cause

If your child shows any of these signs, or if you have other reasons to believe that your child may be overprogrammed, then drop one or more of these extracurricular activities.

After you have determined a specific time (or times) for homework sessions, you're ready for the next step: determining how that time should be organized. Here are some parent-tested recommendations:

1. Encourage your child to start each homework session by looking over everything that needs to be done. Ask, "Which parts can you do on your own? Which parts will you need help with?"

2. Suggest that your child do the most difficult or distasteful task first, before fatigue sets in. There's nothing worse than being asked to explain a complicated math problem when both you and your child are ready to call it a day.

3. When homework involves memorizing information or reviewing for a test, this should be done early in the session, while both you and your child are fresh. Then, at the end of the session, go over the material one more time. If possible, review it again in the morning before school.

Help!

"I get home from work just in time to fix dinner. My daughter has gymnastics after school and eats dinner as soon as she gets home. Both of us are exhausted afterward. How can we possibly fit homework in?"

Your case is an exception to our "do-the-hardest-homework-first" rule. You may want to try letting your daughter do her easiest homework in the evening, before bedtime. Then, depending on how much homework she has, have her get up half an hour earlier in the morning, dress and eat breakfast, and complete the more difficult work before leaving for school.

"My son does his homework as long as there isn't anything interesting on TV. If there is, I have to nag him to do it."

What's wrong with exercising some parental control? Decide on a specific number of hours per day (preferably one at the most) during which your son is allowed to watch television. Have him tell you which programs he wants to watch, and either give your approval or suggest something else. And make it a rule that in order to watch his programs, he must finish his homework first. He'll probably scream and yell and argue, but stand firm; once he learns that you mean business, he'll settle down—and buckle down.

> **"My son has a habit of springing big projects on us. We find out at the last minute that he has a report or project to do. Then, we all have to scramble to help him out of a hole at the eleventh hour."**

Post a calendar in your son's room or study area. Work with him to identify holidays, special events, and times for extracurricular activities. Then add in due dates for big projects. Show your son how to do "backward planning" and work on small tasks toward a larger goal or final product.

How to set up a home study center

Deciding where your child should do homework is as important as deciding when it should be done. A good study center includes certain basic features. Beyond these, be creative in designing a study area to suit the needs of your child's learning style. Here are some points to consider:

LIGHTING

Good lighting is always important, but some children prefer brighter lights than others. Set up a desk lamp at the table or desk where your child works.

SEATING

Good posture helps concentration. This isn't to say that your child can't slump into a beanbag chair to read a story, but for optimum attention to homework, a straight-backed chair at a table or desk is best.

NOISE

Although some children can study in the midst of TVs and radios blaring, other children playing, dogs barking, and parents conversing, it's better if the study center is relatively quiet. If possible, it should be located away from where distracting toys are kept. A "Do Not Disturb" sign can be a nice touch.

STUDY MATERIALS

Often the first few minutes of homework time are wasted as children search the house for materials they need. You can put an end to this by stocking the home study center with writing instruments, erasers, paper, note cards, paper clips, pencil sharpeners, correction fluid, and other supplies. Make a small chalkboard or dry-erase board available for exercises that would normally be done on scratch paper, and hang a bulletin board for posting calendars, important notices, and directions for special projects.

A COMPUTER

Computers are becoming more and more common in the home. Computers are helpful for accessing information for reports and projects, completing writing assignments, and practicing basic skills in reading and mathematics. If you decide to include a computer in your child's home study center (or if you allow him to use the family computer), you'll also need supplies such as printer paper, ink cartridges, blank CDs or disks, and computer software. See Chapter 9 for more detailed information about homework and computers.

CAUTION

When you're making the decision about where to set up your child's study area, also think about whether this is where you want to set up a computer with Internet access. If your child will be allowed to surf the Internet without your direct supervision, set up the computer in a central place in your home, so you and others can easily see what your child is viewing and doing online.

REFERENCE MATERIALS

The study center should include a small reference library. For children in kindergarten and first grade, a "pictionary," or picture dictionary, is a good idea. For children above first grade level, supply a dictionary written at a level your child can understand. Check your local bookstore; good dictionaries for students are published by HarperCollins, Houghton Mifflin, Simon & Schuster, and Merriam-Webster. You might also want to select a thesaurus for your child; HarperCollins, Simon & Schuster, and Merriam-Webster all publish reputable student thesauruses. A set of encyclopedias saves trips to the library; the *World Book* is an excellent resource for older elementary school children, since it's easier to read than most other encyclopedias. An atlas and a globe can also be useful. If you have a computer, consider purchasing an encyclopedia or dictionary on CD-ROM, or buy an online subscription to an encyclopedia such as *World Book* or *Encyclopedia Britannica*. Multimedia reference works are becoming more readily available (and affordable); interactive encyclopedias and video almanacs can bring learning to life for your child. If you have Internet access, encyclopedias, dictionaries, almanacs, and other searchable reference materials are easily accessible.

YOUR PRESENCE

Generally speaking, the younger the child, the more likely it is that he will get down to work if you're nearby. You shouldn't have to hover over him during every homework session, but if he's at the kitchen table while you're preparing dinner, or at the dining room table while you're reading the newspaper in the next room, the opportunities for distraction will be fewer. And you'll be around to answer questions and provide encouragement. Older children with a proven track record of doing their homework without constant supervision can be allowed to study in their room or another place of their choosing, as long as it meets the criteria previously outlined.

20 tips for homework helpers

1. Maintain two-way communication with your child.

Don't just lecture. Listen and respond to what your child has to say. When you respond, don't plead or argue. (Pleading puts your child in charge; arguing creates a no-win situation.) Instead, respond assertively and positively.

2. Don't give your child a choice unless you mean it.

Instead of saying, "Would you like to work on your science homework now?" say, "It's time to work on your science homework. Please join me at the table." Or, if you really want to offer a choice between two tasks, phrase it in a way that's likely to get the desired response. *Example:* "You can do your science homework now or after dinner. But if you wait until after dinner, we won't have time to go to the park."

3. Set goals with, not for, your child. Then focus on one at a time.

Start with a goal that your child is almost guaranteed to achieve. That will make the others more appealing and continued success more likely.

4. Expect progress.

We all respond to the expectations other people have of us. (This is known as the self-fulfilling prophecy syndrome.) If your expectations are low, your child's achievements are likely to match them. If your expectations are high *but not unreasonable,* your child will respond in kind.

5. Make your child aware of her improvement. Reward achievement.

Don't "pay" for every accomplishment with a treat or a promise. Often it's enough simply to say, "You did a really good job on that map. I'm proud of you." But if your child works especially hard on a challenging assignment and completes it successfully, that's worth celebrating.

6. Praise generously, yet honestly.

Praise will lose its effectiveness if used indiscriminately, plus, a child can usually tell when you're not being sincere.

7. Direct praise to the task at hand.

Saying, "You spelled eight out of ten words right. Much better!" is more specific than "Good for you!" Specific praise guides future behavior.

8. Try not to show disappointment if your child doesn't do as well as you'd like.

Look for your child's strengths; avoid criticism. The child whose performance is poor doesn't need reminding; she needs encouragement and reassurance that you value her *regardless of her performance.*

9. Be enthusiastic. Use humor.

Starting every homework session with the *Star Wars* theme might be going overboard. But it doesn't hurt to smile and say, "I like spending this time with you." And you don't have to be deadly serious about it. Laughter, shared jokes, and even a tickle or two can go a long way toward lightening the homework load.

10. Use timers and competition wisely.

For some children, a timer spurs effort and ends stalling; for others, it's anxiety-producing. If the latter seems true for your child, put the timer away. Some children enjoy competing against themselves and trying to better their past achievements, and if this is the case with your child, that's fine. But competition with friends, brothers, or sisters can be threatening and debilitating, especially if the child is at an academic disadvantage.

11. Be prepared to teach.

Even though the teacher is responsible for teaching the subject matter, this doesn't always happen, and you may need to "fill in the blanks." Skimming the textbook and carefully reading lesson materials and handouts will prepare you for this role.

12. Use concrete, hands-on materials whenever possible, especially (but not exclusively) when working with a young child.

For example, it's easier to learn 2 + 3 with blocks than with pictures. And for most people, it's easier to learn with pictures than with numbers.

13. Help your child build associations between what she already knows and what is being learned.

Children learn new concepts by recognizing how they are like and different from concepts they already know. *Examples:* "Multiplying fractions is like regular multiplying except . . ." "A stream is like the canal behind Grandma's house except . . ." "The electrons in an atom circle the proton. What circles the sun?" A child who mentally pictures the solar system has a better understanding of what goes on in an atom.

14. Provide adequate practice.

Children shouldn't just learn material; they should actually *overlearn* it to promote the development of long-term memory. Try to ignore complaints of "We already did that! This is boring!" But don't run a subject or a concept into the ground. Know when to stop.

15. Provide variety.

If a child starts fidgeting excessively over a math book, switch to spelling for a while. Return to math later. In between, share a snack, take a short walk, or have a joke-telling session.

16. Encourage creativity.

Although you should be careful about "sticking to the rules," a certain amount of creativity can "help the medicine go down." A story in one of the basal readers (reading textbooks) tells of a child whose Thanksgiving homework assignment was to make a Pilgrim doll. The child's mother was an Eastern European immigrant. The child dressed the doll in Russian attire, and the doll served as a lesson to the class that the United States has had many kinds of pilgrims over the years.

17. Encourage independence.

For example, if your child is able to read directions independently, encourage her to do so.

18. Take every opportunity to build your child's self-esteem.

This includes, but isn't confined to, most of the other tips already presented here. Use your imagination and your natural affection and concern to think of other ways to show your child that she is a worthwhile and important person.

19. Check with the teacher before correcting your child's homework.

Many teachers want to see a student's mistakes; they use them to determine where more teaching is called for. A perfect parent-corrected paper can be misleading and can rob a child of the extra help she may need.

20. Show a positive attitude toward school.

If you have problems with your child's school or teacher, don't discuss them with the child. Instead, show your respect for school by emphasizing the importance of regular attendance, a neat appearance, and grades that reflect your child's true capabilities. Then make an appointment to speak privately with the teacher.

Troubleshooting

If you have difficulties working with your child…

Experience has already shown you that parenting isn't easy. Whenever you make a change in the way you relate to your child, you can expect problems to surface at some point along the way. Deciding to help with homework will change the way you relate to your child. He may resist your help at first—or accept it initially and resist it later. Your best-laid plans may founder on the realities of temper tantrums and power struggles.

What can you do if you have difficulties working with your child? First, try not to assume that any and all homework-related problems are the fault of your child, the teacher, or the school. A surprising number may trace back to *your own* experiences and behaviors. There's nothing unusual about this; even parents aren't perfect! The point is, these problems *can* be solved. All it takes is willingness on your part to examine your expectations and behaviors and modify those that aren't working.

Remind yourself of these simple yet essential truths: You are an adult; your child is still a child. You have years of experience to draw on; your child is relatively new to the world. You are capable of problem solving, analyzing, and reasoning; your child may not have developed these skills yet. Also, your child is counting on you to be older and wiser, to set rules and boundaries, and to offer guidance when and where it's needed. Often the more a child rebels and resists, the more that child is crying out for parents to take charge. When you say, "You *will* do your homework, and that's final," you're not being mean or unfair—you're being a parent! And the more firm and consistent you are, the easier it will become and the more responsive your child will be.

The following issues come up again and again when parents talk about the difficulties they have in working with their children. Exploring these issues here may help you to avoid them or deal with them effectively should they arise.

Help!

? **"My parents never had trouble getting me to do my homework. I can't understand why my child is so stubborn about it."**

Are you treating your child the way your parents treated you? There are two reasons why this may be backfiring: You aren't your parents, and your child isn't you.

Even though most parents vow that they will never treat their children as their parents treated them, research has shown that we tend to repeat our parents' behaviors. It's perfectly fine to draw on the wisdom you gained from your mother and father—as long as you also leave room for your own good sense and instincts. And keep an open mind to what today's experts are saying about how children learn. Much of this information was unavailable to your parents, and we can all stand to benefit from it. For suggestions on books you may want to read, see pages 139–141.

? **"I don't have any trouble working with other people's children. Why is it so hard with mine?"**

Many parents can do a good job of teaching children—as long as they're not their own. There are many reasons for this. To begin with, you're usually not as emotionally attached to other people's children. Your expectations aren't as high. Your ego isn't as involved.

When working with your own child, you may find it hard to maintain a balance between being interested and being pushy. We all want to encourage our children to do their best. It's an almost irresistible parental urge. But it's far more effective to be genuinely *interested* in what they are doing, what they are experiencing, what they are feeling, and what their needs are. Being interested means putting them first, listening to what they have to say, and tailoring your responses to what's best for them.

You may discover that your emotions interfere with your teaching. While honesty is usually the best policy, there are times when it's best to conceal your true feelings for the sake of your child's self-esteem. For example, no child functions well in the face of parental disappointment or anger. Rather than show these feelings, take a break. Go off by yourself to cool down, or do something fun with your child. You'll both feel better.

Take time to examine your goals for your child. Do you see your child as an extension of yourself? Do you see your child as a reflection of your parenting abilities? Do you want your child to achieve everything you didn't or couldn't achieve when you were in school? Are you subconsciously trying to "keep up with the Joneses" through your child's accomplishments? Remember that your child is a unique individual—one of a kind, and one in a million. The more you project this attitude, the more your child may achieve. The freedom to be oneself is a powerful motivator.

❓ **"I must have gone over this material a thousand times! Why can't my child get it?"**

Many parents find teachers amazing. "I don't know how you do it. I'd never have the patience to be a teacher," they say. So you didn't become a teacher—and here you are, forced to teach anyway! If it's any consolation, even the best teachers get impatient. As long as you recognize your impatience and can deal with it effectively, don't let it concern you. It's normal, natural, and inevitable.

The only time to worry is when your lack of patience (or your emotional involvement, expectations, or ego) seriously hampers your ability to help your child. If it becomes clear to you that you're not the best person for the job, find someone else. Many parents hire professional tutors for their children. (For more on this topic, see pages 30–32.)

❓ **"I work crazy hours and can't always supervise my child's homework."**

If your child needs homework supervision and no one is available to provide it at home, make an alternate plan. Call or visit your child's teacher, explain your situation, and ask for suggestions. It's possible to provide supervision under all kinds of circumstances; it just takes some planning.

How to learn how your child thinks and learns

Each of us has both strengths and challenges in learning. We're just naturally better at some things than others. Part of becoming a successful student is learning how to emphasize what we do well and cope with areas of learning that are more difficult. You can help your child do just that—discover her strengths and find ways to work through more difficult tasks. The best way to learn how your child thinks and learns is by observing her and talking with her.

You may discover that your child learns material best in a way that is different from how you learn or different from how you would ordinarily approach a task. Some people are visual learners—they see and they remember. Some people are auditory learners—they hear and they remember. Some people are kinesthetic, or tactile, learners—they learn by touching, feeling, and moving. Some people are "combos"—they learn with multiple pathways. Think of ways to build on your child's learning strengths. For example, in learning spelling words, if your child is a visual learner, make spelling flash cards. Have your child read the flash cards several times, and then take a practice spelling test. If your child is an auditory learner, go over the words with a "mock spelling bee" and then take a practice test. If your child is a kinesthetic learner, have her write the words or type the words several times and then take a practice test. If your child is a combo learner, try all of the above.

Finally, if you can't get a handle on how your child learns best and if you have concerns about your child's progress in school, talk with your child's teacher to get some ideas. After consulting with the teacher, you may decide to have your child tested either privately or through a school psychologist to learn more about her strengths and challenges in learning.

Differentiation in the classroom

Teachers today are becoming better trained in assessing individual student needs and responding to those needs in appropriate ways. While there are many definitions of differentiated instruction, Tracey Hall, Ph.D., provides one that is particularly helpful: "To differentiate instruction is to recognize students' varying background knowledge, readiness, language, preference in learning, interests, and to react responsively. Differentiated instruction is a process to approach teaching and learning for students with differing abilities in the same class."* In other words, teachers now adjust the pace, style, and level of instruction to meet the needs of individual students in their class. The goal is to provide quality instruction for all students. Ask your child's teacher if he or she is differentiating instruction in the classroom and *how* he or she is differentiating for your child.

Types of intelligence

Parents often feel that their children are the "best and the brightest," regardless of their grades or score on an IQ test. In fact, the Theory of Multiple Intelligences, developed by Dr. Howard Gardner of Harvard University, suggests that there are many different ways of being "smart." Gardner has identified eight areas of intelligence: linguistic, musical, logical/mathematical, spatial, bodily/kinesthetic, interpersonal, intrapersonal, and naturalist. The idea is that we all possess each type of intelligence, just to varying degrees.

The book *You're Smarter Than You Think: A Kid's Guide to Multiple Intelligences*, by Dr. Thomas Armstrong, discusses these different types of intelligence and provides practical suggestions for building on strengths and coping with difficult learning tasks. Here's how Dr. Armstrong describes each type of intelligence.* You may want to use these descriptions to talk with your child about interests and strengths.

1. Word smart (linguistic intelligence): You like words and how they're used in reading, writing, or speaking. You may enjoy word play and word games, foreign languages, storytelling, spelling, creative writing, or reading.

2. Music smart (musical intelligence): You appreciate music, rhythm, melody, and patterns in sounds. You are capable of

---

*Tracey Hall, Ph.D., "Differentiated Instruction," National Center on Accessing the General Curriculum, *www.cast.org/ncac/ DifferentiatedInstruction2876.cfm* (accessed October 8, 2004).

hearing tone and pitch. You may appreciate many different kinds of music and enjoy activities like singing, playing instruments, listening to CDs, or attending concerts.

3. Logic smart (logical-mathematical intelligence): You enjoy figuring things out and may understand numbers and math concepts, like finding patterns, and have fun with science. You may like riddles, brainteasers, computers, creating your own codes, or doing science experiments.

4. Picture smart (spatial intelligence): You love to look at the world and see all the interesting things in it. You may be able to picture things or images in your head. You may be able to take what you see and use your imagination to show others your vision through art, design, photography, architecture, or invention.

5. Body smart (bodily-kinesthetic intelligence): You're graceful and comfortable in your body, using it to learn new skills or to express yourself in different ways. You may be an athlete or use your body artistically in dance or acting. Or you may have more interest in working with your hands and doing activities like crafts, building models, or repairing things.

6. People smart (interpersonal intelligence): You're interested in other people and how people interact with each other. You may be part of student government or a peer mediation group at school, have lots of friends, be involved in neighborhood causes, or just enjoy being in casual social groups.

7. Self smart (intrapersonal intelligence): You're aware of and understand your own feelings, what you're good at, and the areas you want to improve. You often understand yourself better than others understand you. You may keep a journal, create plans for the future, reflect on the past, or set goals for yourself.

8. Nature smart (naturalist intelligence): You're observant and enjoy identifying and classifying things like plants, animals, or rocks. (If you live in the city, you may classify other things like CDs or what your classmates wear.) You probably love being outdoors and may be interested in gardening, taking care of pets, cooking, or getting involved in ecological causes.

Help!

"I have been reading about learning styles and multiple intelligences. My son is definitely a spatial learner. How can I encourage his teachers to create lessons that are more aligned with his way of learning?"

Chances are that your child's teacher does not have the time or inclination to individualize learning for your son. On the other hand, his teacher may appreciate knowing your insights about how he learns best. The teacher may be willing to supplement verbal lectures with demonstrations or visual supplements to help your son and all learners in the classroom. He or she may also have suggestions on how you can structure homework sessions to be consistent with what is being taught in the classroom while being sensitive to your son's highly visual orientation.

"My son is in fifth grade and has been identified for gifted education services. He is pretty sharp, but his grades don't show it."

While your son may be bright, he may be feeling bored or unchallenged in class, he may be feeling too much pressure to do well and just stop trying altogether, or he may need to work on his organizational skills and study habits. Talk with your son's teacher about his underachievement. Find out if your son finds his schoolwork too easy, too repetitive, or generally uninteresting or if your son is just trying to get out of doing his work. Teach your child strategies for dealing with boredom or how to be better organized and stay on top of his assignments (see the column to the right for more ideas about this).

"My daughter has a learning disability. She has particular difficulty learning to read. She's in fifth grade and still reads on a first-grade level. Homework time is crying time at our house."

Talk with your daughter's teacher about her homework plan and ask if the school offers any programs or extra support for students with learning difficulties. Explain that you want to help but need to find a way to make her educational activities at home enjoyable and productive while still supporting what is going on in school. In the meantime, stay positive with your daughter and remind her of what she does well. You can talk about multiple intelligences and help her realize that she is smart and capable in many ways. Also, Gary Fisher and Rhoda Cummings have written *The Survival Guide for Kids with LD* (Free Spirit Publishing, 2002). After reading this book, talk to your daughter about ways to cope with a learning difference.

How to help your child keep track of assignments

All homework starts life as an assignment, given by a teacher to a child. Unfortunately, many assignments get lost, misplaced, or misunderstood somewhere between school and home. Unless you live in the Bermuda Triangle, there's really no reason why assignments can't arrive home in the same condition they left school. All it takes is a few new habits—and a few useful organization tools.

A BOOK BAG OR BACKPACK

A book bag or backpack is an absolute must where homework is concerned. Your child's bag should be prepared every night before school and left in a convenient, regular place for pickup in the morning.

Shopping for a book bag or backpack can be an enjoyable parent-child outing. As much as possible, respect your child's wishes where style is concerned; certain bags may be "in" at school, while others are definitely "out." An unpopular bag stands an excellent chance of "disappearing." (Also check to see if your child's school has any restrictions concerning book bags. For example, some schools ban backpacks with wheels, as these type of bags are often too big to fit in student lockers.)

A particular word of caution needs to be made regarding book bag or backpack safety.

A bag (loaded) should weigh no more than 10 percent of your child's body weight. It's worth the investment to buy a bag made of quality, lightweight material and one that has two broad, sturdy straps. Encourage your child not to sling the pack over one shoulder—it's important to use both straps and to center the weight on the back.

NOTEBOOKS

Children should have notebooks that make it easy to get organized and stay organized. Large loose-leaf binders with subject separators, envelopes for loose papers, and pencil cases can encourage a child to keep supplies and assignments in order. It's harder to lose or forget a loose-leaf binder than a series of thin individual folders.

Again, let your child participate in the buying decision. Many children love to pick out their own notebooks and pencil cases, put things neatly where they belong, and show off their new acquisitions to their friends.

Shopping for supplies can also be an opportunity to add any "extras" to your child's home study center. Pick up a stapler, a tape dispenser, a paper punch, and a ruler; label them with your child's name and declare them "hands-off" to the rest of the family. Little touches like these mean a lot to a child.

A STUDENT PLANNER OR CALENDAR

Many loose-leaf binders come equipped with school-year (or all-year) calendars. If your child's doesn't, consider purchasing a teacher's planning calendar (available in school and office supplies stores) for recording short-term and long-term assignments.

Or buy a student planner or calendar; many schools today have their own planners that they provide to students or require students to buy. If your child's school doesn't have its own planner, several companies now offer them, and they really do help.

For the technology-oriented, you may want to consider a personal digital assistant (PDA). Handheld PDA devices can house software for keeping track of assignments and due dates, tracking grades, and storing information such as emails and addresses.

Examples of Planning Tools:

- **Day-Timer Student Planner.** Student Planner, designed by students for students, helps them balance school, work, friends, activities, and more, so they can enjoy life and stay focused on what's important. Features weekly dated pages and monthly tabbed calendars. Day-Timers, Inc. • 1 Willow Lane • East Texas, PA 18046 • 1-800-457-5702 • *www.daytimer.com*

- *Handmark 4.0 Student CD-ROM.* Software for PDA devices that enables students to keep track of coursework, assignments, grades, and calendar. palmOne • 400 North McCarthy Boulevard • Milpitas, CA 95035 • *www.palmone.com*

- **Premier Discover Agendas.** Colorful agendas for elementary and middle school students. Useful for planning weekly goals and daily "to do's." Premier Headquarters • 2000 Kentucky Street • Bellingham, WA 98229 • 1-800-447-2034 • *www.premier.us*

ASSIGNMENT SHEETS

Your child's teacher may provide these. If not, feel free to make several photocopies of the sample assignment sheets on pages 144 and 145. Slip these into your child's loose-leaf binder just ahead of the calendar; then make sure they're kept up-to-date throughout the school year. Check the sheets often early in the year, less often as your child begins to take responsibility for this task.

Help!

? **"My son's school backpack and notebook are a mess! Papers are stuffed everywhere, and he can never find a thing."**

Schoolbags and notebooks can become portable trash bins. Your son needs help organizing his. After the first major cleanup (done with your assistance), have him start each evening study session with a five-minute "tidy time." Supervise, but don't do it for him. Eventually he'll form the habit and organize his materials on his own. It takes time to make life simple. Taking just a few minutes to put things in order can save lots of time and anxiety later on.

? **"My daughter forgets her homework on purpose so she won't have to do it."**

Your course of action will depend on the reason your daughter is "forgetting" her homework. Here are some possible causes to consider and solutions to try:

1. She may be seeking attention. Even "negative attention"—including displeasure and scoldings—qualifies as attention. Skip the scenes and calmly let her know that you'll work with her if she brings her homework home, but you'll pay little attention to her if she doesn't. Then follow through! When she starts "remembering" her homework (which she will), give her the positive attention you promised.

2. The homework may be too difficult for her. Confer with the teacher to determine whether your daughter is capable of handling the assignments. If she isn't, try to find out why. Is she having trouble paying attention in class or grasping new concepts? Does she need extra help? Does she lack self-confidence? Let the teacher make suggestions about what to do, and don't hesitate to contribute suggestions of your own. *Examples:* Maybe your daughter needs to be shown that (with a minimum of help) she can do assignments she thought were too difficult. Or perhaps the teacher can give her easier assignments until she's ready to handle more difficult ones. Or maybe the assignments can be broken up into smaller, more manageable pieces. (See also the discussion on differentiation in the classroom on page 20.)

3. Your daughter may not recognize the importance of her homework assignments. Quite often, children don't understand why homework is assigned or how doing homework (or not doing it) affects their grades. Arrange for a three-way meeting with your daughter, her teacher, and you. Ask the teacher to explain the purpose for homework in his or her class, how it is scored, and how it factors into the final grade.

4. Your daughter may be just plain lazy. It's not very flattering, but it may be true!

Start by requiring your daughter to record all of her assignments on an assignment sheet. Ask the teacher to initial the sheet daily to show that an assignment has been given, and also to initial it whenever homework is handed in. Insist on seeing the sheet every evening. (You may want to tie this to a privilege or two. *Examples:* No sheet, no TV. Or no sheet, no after-school bike rides.)

Whenever your daughter neglects to bring home the materials needed to complete an assignment, give her an alternate homework assignment or an uninteresting chore to do. Or you might try a tactic that some parents have used with success: Collect her incomplete homework on Fridays and have her spend time over the weekend finishing it. When homework starts seriously interfering with play, most children see the light.

"My son *never* brings handouts home. As a result, we never know about PTA meetings or other school functions until it's too late. And if he is given a worksheet to complete at home, it never arrives and he receives a zero on the assignment. Anything handed out in class is lost forever!"

This is a common problem. (It's amazing how children can sort through the various handouts they receive in class and manage to bring home *only* those that have to do with field trips!) Encourage your son to put all handouts in his loose-leaf binder as soon as they are given out in class. Emphasize that he is *not* to stuff them in his desk or locker, the Black Holes of the grade school set.

Post a chart on the refrigerator. Whenever your son brings home a handout (whether an announcement or a worksheet), give him a star, a check mark, or a sticker. Reward him once a certain number has been reached. Or you might give your son a special folder just for handouts. Let him decorate it with crayons, markers, or stickers. Ask to see the folder every evening.

As a last resort, send your son's teacher several self-addressed, stamped envelopes to be used for mailing handouts home. This may seem like giving up or giving in, but there's a catch: Have your son pay for the postage out of his allowance. This is almost guaranteed to get fast results! Also, check with your child's teacher about the possibility of receiving important announcements via email.

"My son has been complaining about backaches. I think it might be due to his backpack, which is always overloaded. Is this something he'll grow out of?"

Don't ignore your child's physical symptoms. Get him checked out by your family physician. Children often carry their bags improperly, which can lead to long-term injuries. Also, follow the guidelines on pages 22–23 for better backpack safety.

How to help your child prepare for regular classroom tests

Schools don't typically teach children how to study for tests. Some children manage well regardless, but others need step-by-step guidance. Here are some suggestions you can use to help your child prepare for tests, eliminate night-before panics, and lessen test anxiety.

BEFORE THE TEST

1. Find out the teacher's system for scheduling tests. Some tests might be given on a regular basis (*example:* spelling tests every Friday). Others might be more irregular or incidental (*example:* social studies tests when a chapter or unit is completed). On the day the test is announced (and provided that your child tells you about it), work with your child to plan a study schedule that doesn't leave everything for the last minute.

2. Encourage your child to study "actively." Children who underline key words in the text (if this is allowed), take notes, and write outlines while reading are more likely to do well than those who merely let their eyes wander down the page.

3. Have your child invent questions that seem likely to appear on the test. Then have him try to answer the questions. This will point out areas of study that need more attention and review.

4. Teach your child the "STAR" test-taking strategy. This is particularly useful for timed tests, although it can also be applied to untimed tests.

> **S**urvey the test to see which items can be answered quickly.
>
> **T**ake time to read the directions carefully.
>
> **A**nswer the questions you can answer quickly, leaving difficult items for last.
>
> **R**eread the questions and your answers, making any needed corrections.

5. Reassure your child that it's okay to leave answers blank or guess answers if he doesn't know them or can't figure them out. Some children are reluctant to go on to the next question; they get stuck midway, and their grades suffer as a result. Your child may need to practice this on untimed tests before attempting it on timed tests.

6. Make sure that your child is well rested and fed on the morning of the test. If time allows, you may want to take him out to breakfast so he will have pleasant associations with the day.

AFTER THE TEST

1. Talk to your child about the test. Which parts were easy? Which parts were difficult?

2. When the graded test is handed back, work with your child to analyze any errors. Try to determine why each error was made. Was it a careless mistake? Was information omitted when your child was studying for the test? Did he forget something covered during the study session?

3. File the test and any notes or outlines made prior to the test. These can be valuable references and study tools for later cumulative tests.

For more information on helping your child prepare for tests, see pages 94–95 and 107–110.

Help!

? **"My daughter either doesn't study for tests or informs me of a test at 9 p.m. the night before—right when she's supposed to go to bed."**

Teach her how to complete an assignment sheet, with descriptions of assignments (including tests) and due dates. Go over the sheet with her on a weekly basis and use it to plan study time. Use the "Before the test" guidelines on page 26 to help her form new and/or improved study habits.

"My son crams for tests the night before and does moderately well, but he forgets the material before final exams."

First, he shouldn't be cramming—he should be studying well in advance of each test. Second, it's clear that your son needs to periodically review material he has already learned. Go over past tests with him. Look back at former worksheets, papers, and reports. He needs to understand that learning is a *process,* not a series of individual units to be memorized now and discarded later.

"My daughter just 'freaks' during tests. The night before a test she can hardly sleep. Then when she takes a test, she freezes."

Some test anxiety is good—it can serve as a motivator to study and be well-prepared. On the other hand, too much test anxiety can cause both physical and mental distress. Follow the steps for reducing test anxiety on pages 109–110. If you don't see progress, discuss the situation with your daughter's teacher or school counselor to get additional support.

How to help your child prepare for high-stakes tests

In 2001, the United States Congress reauthorized the 1965 Elementary and Secondary Education Act naming it the No Child Left Behind Act *(www.nclb.gov).* The act requires states to implement standardized testing in reading, mathematics, writing, and eventually science. Conducted annually, these tests are based on curriculum standards adopted by each state. They are frequently called "high-stakes" tests because test results have implications for students, teachers, administrators, and schools. Students who do not pass standardized tests may be held back a grade or fail to graduate. Low test scores are considered when teachers and administrators receive job performance reviews. Schools can be "graded" based on test scores— grades can be used to make personnel and budget decisions. Stakes are high and getting higher.

There is a great deal of controversy about standardized tests. Advocates feel that the tests encourage schools to set higher standards and to be more accountable for student learning. Critics argue that testing takes away from subject areas other than those tested and that teachers are forced to teach to the test. Whether you are pro or con, the tests are a reality of public education. Your job as a parent is fourfold:

- First, learn about what high-stakes testing means for your child. You can find information about testing schedules, implications, and test formats at most state education Web sites. If your child is an English language learner or a child who qualifies for special education services, make certain that you understand the policies and procedures for your child.

- Second, ensure that your child is prepared academically. Talk with your child's teacher about what you can do to support your child's learning. Ask if the school or state has some online activities for test preparation.

- Third, help your child prepare psychologically and physically for the test. Try to help reduce anxiety and encourage your child to do her best. Make certain that your child gets enough sleep the night before the test and has a good breakfast the day of testing.

- Fourth, do not hesitate to ask your child's teachers how to interpret your child's test scores.

Additional suggestions for helping your child prepare for high-stakes tests are included in Chapter 8.

To bribe or not to bribe?

Teachers talk a lot about "behavior modification," "rewarding children for appropriate behavior," and "withholding rewards" (or imposing unpleasant consequences) for inappropriate behavior. These may sound like descriptions of the age-old practice known as bribery.

Should you bribe your child to do homework? The answer is yes—and no. We all respond to rewards. Few adults would show up at work if they weren't paid to do so. Most of us trust that certain actions will lead to expected rewards, whether personal (feeling good about ourselves), social (being thanked or praised by others), or material (receiving a concrete reward). Similarly, we realize that other actions will lead to less pleasant personal, social, or material consequences.

Children's actions should also lead to consequences that are clearly spelled out ahead of time. When you set consequences, make sure that *you* can live with them! In setting consequences, what you're really doing is giving your child a choice. If your child chooses the consequence for not doing homework, then you must impose it with no anger, pleading, or hesitation on your part.

Most children aren't mature enough to value personal rewards, so they need more tangible external motivation. It's preferable that this take the form of social rather than material rewards (or unpleasant consequences). But if the only motivation a child will respond to is material, then you shouldn't hesitate to use this option. Just remember to gradually phase it out when it's no longer needed.

Children who are hard to motivate require frequent rewards. For this to have the desired effect, it's important that the rewards be *consistent* and appropriate to what you want the child to do. (Of course, any punishments should meet these same criteria.) Buying your child an expensive toy for completing an assignment is *not* an appropriate reward. Grounding your child for a month for failing to complete an assignment is *not* an appropriate punishment.

It's usually best to offer small rewards for achieving short-term goals, and equally small punishments for not achieving them. (*Examples:* You might award a colorful sticker or a quarter for doing an assignment, or withhold a privilege for not doing it.) Wait until later to set equivalent rewards and punishments for achieving (or not achieving) long-term goals. Once you decide on a system of rewards and consequences, you may want to use a contract to formalize the arrangement. Consider letting your child design the contract.

Help!

"My son finds any number of excuses to leave his homework and do something else. As a result, it often takes him all evening to complete an assignment that should take half an hour. I have lectured him, and I have praised him when he's been at least moderately attentive. But neither of these approaches seems to work."

Try providing him with concrete rewards for completing his homework within a reasonable amount of time. (*Example:* If he enjoys riding his scooter or skateboard, you can use this as a reward.) Since you don't want to give him an excuse to fail, make your initial requirements fairly easy to satisfy. Let him ride for half an hour after finishing half of his homework. Later in the evening, when the other half is done, allow him additional riding time.

"My eleven-year-old daughter does her homework, but only when I prompt her. How can I eliminate the need for constant scolding?"

You can decide to *stop* reminding—effective immediately. And you can end an ongoing power struggle that isn't very satisfying for you or your daughter. You may think that when you scold your daughter and she does her homework, you're the winner of the power struggle. In fact, you're the loser. Your daughter has figured out precisely how much "pushing" it takes to send you over the edge into anger. When you react to her pushing by scolding, you are actually letting her control the situation!

Remember that *you're the adult*—you're supposed to be smarter and stronger than she is. You can choose to ignore her pushing and focus calmly on the task at hand. Figure out a reward that would mean something to her, and use it to provoke the response you want to see. *Example:* If your daughter enjoys going to movies on the weekends, tell her she can—as long as she does her homework. Allow some room for failure until the new pattern has been established. Let her know that if she completes three out of four days of homework assignments, you'll give her the money for a movie ticket. Eventually you can increase that to four days out of four.

If you disagree with a teacher about homework...

Perhaps you feel that your child is being assigned too much homework or too little, or homework that's too hard or too easy, or homework that takes too much time or not enough to complete. Whenever you're dissatisfied with or uncertain about any aspect of your child's education, these are the steps to take:

1. Make an appointment to talk with your child's teacher.

2. Prepare for your conference by making a list of your questions or concerns. Write them down.

3. Present your questions or concerns to the teacher; then *listen to what the teacher says* in response. Don't hesitate to ask for explanations of any terms or language you don't understand.

4. If you're still dissatisfied when the conference is over, go home and think about it. (This also gives the teacher time to think about the problem and come up with solutions or strategies that may not have occurred to him or her during your meeting.)

5. If the problem persists, make an appointment with the school principal. Follow the same procedure recommended for the teacher conference: Make a list of points you want to cover; then present them at the conference.

For most problems, there is no need to go any further than this in the school hierarchy. For the rare circumstance that does require intervention at a higher level, consult your local board of education representative.

Remember, it's vital to start with your child's teacher. This is the person at school who knows your child best and spends the most time with him. While it may be tempting to go straight to the principal, always give the teacher the first chance to respond.

When and how to hire a tutor

If your child is having difficulty doing homework or other schoolwork, and if for whatever reason you are unable to provide sufficient help yourself, consider seeking professional help in the form of a tutor. Here are some circumstances that might lead you to take this step:

- Your child's teacher or the school counselor recommends it.

- Homework sessions with your child are frequently unpleasant or stressful.

- The rest of your family is suffering because of excessive time spent with one child's homework. (A second child who wants more attention can develop learning problems as a way to get it.)

- Your job hours vary and you're unable to set up a consistent schedule for your child's homework.

- Your child's school problems are severe enough to warrant outside assistance.

If the problem appears to be one of attitude rather than ability, you may want to see a counselor first. But if the causes seem to be academic *and* attitude-related, it's time to look for a tutor. Your child's school system may provide free tutorial services. Start by exploring this option. Otherwise, school administrators may be able to recommend tutors known to them or suggested by other parents or teachers. Your child's teacher may be able to offer advice on the type of training to look for in a tutor.

If you decide to hire a tutor, begin with an in-person interview. Don't make your choice solely on the basis of a telephone conversation. Make sure that you both understand and agree to the following terms and expectations:

1. If the tutoring will take place in your home, you'll resist the urge to "pitch in." You can talk to the tutor briefly before each session begins and after it's over, but stay away while it's going on.

2. You'll be considerate of the tutor's time. If an after-session conference runs half an hour or longer, you'll offer to pay the tutor accordingly.

3. You'll make every effort to provide an environment free of distractions—including bouncy dogs, overheard telephone conversations, curious siblings, and other interruptions.

4. If the tutoring will take place outside your home, you'll have your child at the appointed place regularly and on time. In case of a necessary cancellation, you'll inform the tutor ahead of time. (Make certain you discuss the tutor's policy about payment for canceled sessions.)

5. The tutor and you will agree upon (and put in writing) specific goals to be worked toward with your child. Progress toward these goals will be the primary criterion you'll use in determining whether the tutor's services are satisfactory—and whether you'll continue using and paying for them.

Before the tutor starts working with your child, set up a meeting between you, the tutor, and your child's teacher. This will help the tutor to become oriented to the teacher's routines and expectations. Afterward, the tutor should keep in touch with the teacher. Arrange additional three-way meetings or phone conferences for this, if necessary.

Once the tutoring begins, don't expect miracles overnight. In fact, you should be suspicious of tutors who promise such miracles. Too often, parents who hire tutors in April are disappointed when their children are held back a grade in June. Some children may require tutoring for extended periods of time.

Finally, tutoring should not cause further anxiety. It's normal for a child to be somewhat anxious during the first session. But if anxiety persists after the first few sessions, stop the tutoring. Look for another tutor and try again, or schedule a teacher conference to explore other options.

C A U T I O N

Many parents today are turning to commercial learning centers or chains for tutoring help. These are often well-advertised and promise amazing success; some even offer online tutoring services.

If you're considering a commercial learning center, proceed with caution. Make certain that:

- your child will receive individualized instruction
- the instruction will be based on your child's specific learning needs

- the center is willing to communicate and coordinate with your child's teacher
- you will receive regular updates about your child's progress
- the personnel at the center are highly qualified in terms of teaching credentials and years of experience

What to do when all else fails

Some children absolutely cannot or will not do their homework despite rewards, consequences, promises, or threats, and despite the best and most caring efforts of parents, teachers, tutors, and other concerned persons. If your child's problems resist any and all of the troubleshooting strategies outlined in this chapter, you probably need professional assistance. Ask the teacher about the school's procedures for a psychological evaluation, or seek outside testing. Discuss the results in a conference with the teacher, the school counselor, and the principal.

A change in classroom assignment may be called for. Some children thrive when they are moved to another room at the same grade level; others need more specialized help in the form of a class for learning differences or disabilities. Or the test results may show that a child is being underchallenged and would benefit from a program for gifted students. Or they may indicate the need for a period of psychological counseling.

Try to be objective when studying the alternatives presented to you. Keep in mind your primary purpose: helping your child. With that as your goal, you're certain to make the right decision.

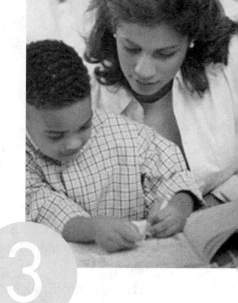

*"Children are made readers
on the laps of their parents."*

EMILIE BUCHWALD

How to Help Your Child with
Reading Words

What's new in reading instruction?

You've seen it on TV. You've read about it in the paper or heard discussions about it on the radio. Reading is a hot topic. In 2000, the National Reading Panel *(www.national readingpanel.org)* published findings from a federally mandated review of reading research. This report showed that reading instruction is most effective when a combination of methods is used, including instruction in phonological awareness (the understanding of speech sounds and manipulation of those sounds to form syllables and words), phonics (the relationships

between sounds and letters), fluency (smooth and easy reading), reading comprehension (understanding what is being read), and vocabulary. The findings of this report coupled with the authorization of the No Child Left Behind Act (see pages 27–28 have changed how reading is taught in many states.

Even with strong national mandates concerning reading instruction, however, the specific methods of teaching children how to read continues to vary from district to district, school to school, and class to class. As a parent, you'll want to find out how your child is being taught to read and how you can best support your child's reading efforts at home. Here are some questions to ask the teacher:

- "Is a reading textbook used? What grade level books are used? Are other reading materials used in the classroom in addition to or instead of a reading textbook?"
- "How are students grouped for reading instruction? How are grouping decisions made?"
- "How is phonological awareness taught?"
- "How is phonics taught?"
- "How is fluency taught?"
- "How is reading comprehension taught?"
- "How is vocabulary taught?"
- "How is my child's progress in reading monitored?"
- "How and when will I be informed if my child is falling behind in reading?"
- "How can I support the reading program by helping at home?"

Since reading opens the door to so many other subjects in school—and to the world of learning in general—it's critical to know when your child is not catching on and to respond quickly. As a parent, you must take responsibility for finding out how your child is being taught and how she is progressing. If your child is not doing well, talk to the teacher and quickly develop a plan for improving the situation.

Even though reading programs vary, there are some ways to help your child that complement any reading program. In this chapter, you'll learn how to read aloud to your child and how to help your child learn phonological awareness, phonics, word patterns, sight words, and longer words.

How to raise your child's reading level

First, you should know that there are three sure ways *not* to raise your child's reading level:

1. Make reading a chore that must be done for a certain amount of time every day, no matter what.

2. Tie your opinion of your child to his reading ability—and communicate that through your attitudes and behaviors.

3. Constantly push your child to read at a higher level.

And there's one sure way to raise your child's reading level—even if that isn't your primary goal:

MAKE READING FUN

If your child grows up loving to read, and that love of reading is at least partly due to your efforts, then you've given your child a gift that will last a lifetime. How can you accomplish this? By keeping this crucial fact in mind at all times: *Reading readiness occurs at different ages, just like the readiness to walk or talk.* Typically, boys are ready later than girls, although this is not always the case. Pushing a child who is not ready can cause irreparable damage by leading to negative attitudes toward reading and a negative self-image.

Of course, this is not to say that children who are ready to read at an earlier age should be prevented from doing so. Some children can sight read words by age three; some can read and comprehend entire books by the time they start kindergarten. If your child is a "born reader," you probably already know this, and you've probably been feeding that eager young mind since you first became aware of its existence.

There is no "magical" point at which every child is ready to read, but there are several factors that indicate readiness:

- the ability to listen and sit still

- an interest in books and in what words say

- good vocabulary and language development

- knowledge of the alphabet

- the ability to discriminate between different letters and sounds

Good "first books" for children to read aloud include picture books, rhymes, and predictable books, all of which children enjoy. (*Examples: Old MacDonald Had a Farm* and some of the simpler Bill Martin Jr. and Dr. Seuss books.) When in doubt about where to start, ask a children's librarian or visit a bookstore that specializes in children's books.

If your child has progressed beyond the beginning reader's stage, your best next step is to ease further progress. Frequent trips to the library, read-aloud sessions, and parent-child conversations on a variety of topics can only heighten an interest in books that is already rooted and growing strong. The more your child reads, the better your child

will read, and you will have helped to raise his reading level by doing the same things you've been doing all along.

During her term as chairperson of the International Reading Association's Parents and Reading Committee, Carole L. Riggs compiled a list of "ABC's" for caring parents. Related to reading and parenting in general, this list is one you should find helpful today and into the future.*

The ABC's of How to Help Your Child

Accept your child unconditionally.

Believe in your child. Trust in his or her ability.

Communicate with your child. Share ideas.

Discuss things with your child.

Enjoy your child. When parents enjoy their children, children enjoy their parents.

Find things of interest to do together.

Give your child responsibility that can be handled. This can lead to a feeling of accomplishment.

Help your child with words of encouragement.

Impress upon your child the vision of what is all around. Talk about the things you see, hear, taste, feel, and smell.

Join your child in fun activities.

Keep from over-identifying with your child. Don't try to live your life again through your child.

Listen to your child. He or she needs someone to share thoughts and ideas.

---

*Reprinted with permission of Carole L. Riggs, Ed.D. "The ABC's of How to Help Your Child." Parent Involvement Packet. Springfield, VA: Personal Press, 1983.

Model behavior you want to see in your child.

Name things for your child. Labels are important.

Observe the way your child goes about tasks. Provide help when needed.

Pace your child. Help your child to do one thing at a time and do it well.

Question your child using question words such as "who," "what," "where," and "when." Ask about stories or everyday things that happen.

Read to your child every day.

Spend time with your child.

Take your child to the library on a regular basis.

Understand that learning isn't always easy. Sometimes we all fail. We can learn from our mistakes.

Value your child's school and teachers. Your attitude will often be mirrored in your child.

Write with your child. Encourage the youngster to write; even scribbles are important.

X is often an unknown quantity. What else would you like to add to this list?

You are your child's most important teacher.

Zip it all up with love. Love gives zest to life.

Here are a few more suggestions about reading:

- Remember that reading *in itself* is not fun. Reading is fun only if you are interested in what you are reading.

- Set aside a time and a place for reading. Allowing children to read past bedtime is one strategy that works well.

- Visit bookstores. If you haven't noticed, bookstores have become "the place to be." You'll find them on Main Street, along the town square, and in shopping malls of all sizes. Book reviews, visiting authors, book clubs, and other special events are scheduled on a regular basis. Some families visit their favorite bookstore once or twice a month as a family outing.

- Don't be limited to books. Reading material is all around us: on cereal boxes, advertisements, signs, recipes, even the backs of buses.

- Provide your child with a book club membership or magazine subscription of his own. For magazine suggestions, see the list on pages 37–38.

- Become familiar with children's books. They seem to be getting better year after year, and they're wonderfully entertaining! (Have you noticed how many celebrities are writing children's books? Jimmy Buffett, Jamie Lee Curtis, Billy Crystal, Jay Leno, and Madonna are among a few examples.) Browse through the children's section of your local library or bookstore and take the time to read some children's books. You're in for a pleasant surprise.

And finally:

- Be a reader yourself. If your child never sees you read, he may conclude that reading is something that is only done in school. If a boy never has a male role model of a teacher, he may conclude that reading is only done by women. When your child asks you what you would like for a birthday or holiday gift, ask for a book—preferably one written by your child.

▮ Resources

Recommended Magazines for Children

Boys' Life • P.O. Box 152079 • Irving, TX 75015 • (972) 580-2366 • *www.boyslife.org*

Published by the Boy Scouts of America since 1911, this monthly magazine for boys ages 6–18 covers everything from science to sports, music, history, pets, entertainment, cars, computers, and health.

Cricket Magazine Group • Carus Publishing Company • P.O. Box 9307 • LaSalle, IL 61301 • 1-800-821-0115 • *www.cricketmag.com*

Cricket Magazine Group offers a line of beautifully illustrated literary publications for children of all ages: *Babybug* (ages 6 months to 2 years); *Ladybug* (ages 2 to 6); *Spider* (ages 6 to 9); *Cricket* (ages 9 to 14); and *Cicada* (ages 14 and up). They teamed up with *Smithsonian* magazine to publish three magazines that nurture a love for the sciences, arts, and humanities: *Click* (ages 3 to 7); *Ask* (ages 7 to 10); and *Muse* (ages 10 and up). Six additional children's magazines focus on history and science: *Appleseeds* (ages 7 to 9); *Cobblestone* (ages 9 to 14); *Faces* (ages 9 to 14); *Calliope* (ages 9 to 14); *Footsteps* (ages 9 to 14); *Odyssey* (ages 10 to 15); and *Dig* (ages 9 to 14).

Highlights for Children • 803 Church Street • Honesdale, PA 18431 • 1-800-255-9517 • *www.highlightsforchildren.com*

For ages 5 to 12, this magazine is dedicated to improving reading skills and helping to define and develop values like honesty, thoughtfulness, and tolerance while also being entertaining and enlightening.

National Geographic Kids • National Geographic Society • 1145 17th Street NW • Washington, DC 20036 • 1-800-647-5463 • *www.nationalgeographic.com/ngkids*

National Geographic Kids is a photo-driven magazine for readers ages 8 to 14. It's an interactive, multi-topic magazine covering animals, entertainment, science, technology, current events, and cultures from around the world.

New Moon • 34 East Superior Street, Suite 200 • Duluth MN 55802 • 1-800-381-4743 • *www.newmoon.org*

This ad-free, multi-cultural magazine is edited by and for girls ages 8 to 14. It offers fiction, poetry, artwork, letters, cartoons, and articles about the lives of girls and women around the globe.

Ranger Rick • National Wildlife Federation • 11100 Wildlife Center Drive • Reston, VA 20190 • 1-800-611-1599 • *www.nwf.org/rangerrick*

Published by the Education Department of the National Wildlife Federation, *Ranger Rick* is a nature magazine for ages 7 and up, filled with stories, photos, and games. Also available from the National Wildlife Federation is *Your Big Backyard* (for ages 3 to 7) and *Wild Animal Baby* (for ages 12 months to 4 years).

Sports Illustrated for Kids • P.O. Box 60001 • Tampa, FL 33660 • 1-800-992-0196 • *www.sikids.com*

Sports Illustrated for Kids is the younger counterpart to *Sports Illustrated* but for ages 8 and up. It offers sports stories, biographies, features, and photos especially for young readers.

For more magazine ideas, ask your local children's librarian for suggestions, or check with a local or online bookstore. Additional magazines are also listed on pages 72–73.

How to read aloud to your child

Reading aloud to your child is the *best* way to help your child learn to read. Start early (from your child's infancy), keep going (well after your child learns how to read), and do it often (daily if possible). The importance of reading aloud to children in terms of their vocabulary acquisition, attitude toward reading, and reading ability cannot be exaggerated. When you read aloud to your child, you:

- model fluent reading
- promote enjoyment and appreciation of children's literature
- develop knowledge of new vocabulary and concepts
- stimulate and motivate independent reading
- develop a bond between you and your child

There are many excellent children's books available in your school or local library. If you need help choosing, ask the librarian, who will be glad to make recommendations and point you toward children's favorites.

As you search for children's literature to share with your child, let her participate actively in this process. Get your child a library card (if you haven't already). Allow her to select at least some of the books you'll be bringing home.

How can you make the most of reading aloud to your child? Here are some suggestions to try before, during, and after:

BEFORE READING ALOUD

- Choose a book you enjoy.
- Choose stories with great characters and good dialogue.
- Relax.
- Set an atmosphere for enjoyment. Find a comfortable chair big enough for two, curl up together on the sofa, or arrange fat pillows on the floor. Make sure that the lighting is adequate for reading and looking at pictures.
- Read the title of the book aloud.
- Read the names of the author and illustrator.
- Look at the cover and skim through the book quickly with your child.
- Start with questions about the subject of the book, your child's experience with that subject, and predictions of what the story might be about.

WHILE READING ALOUD

- Read slowly, but don't "talk down" to your child.
- Create a mood by changing the volume and pitch of your voice.

- Act out parts of the story using puppets or props.
- For younger children, make rhyming books a regular part of your reading sessions. Turn rhymes into games by reading the beginning of each line and letting your child guess the last word.
- Use your sense of humor—laugh a lot!
- Encourage discussion and questions. Allow your child to interrupt you at any point along the way.
- Share personal thoughts with each other about the pictures and story.
- Offer additional information and explain key concepts and vocabulary when your child asks or when you think it is appropriate.

AFTER READING ALOUD

- Ask your child questions about the story.
- Encourage your child to ask you questions about the story. Model how to respond to questions.
- Let your child retell the story in her own words.
- Relate the story to real-life experiences.
- Share personal reactions with each other about likes and dislikes of the story and whether or not you would like to read another book by the same author.

How to help your child with phonological awareness

Effective phonics instruction is built on a strong foundation of *phonological awareness*, the understanding of speech sounds and manipulation of those sounds to form syllables and words. Phonological awareness consists of at least four parts:

- detecting beginning sounds, or onset
- detecting ending sounds, or rhyme
- detecting individual sounds in a whole word, or segmentation
- taking individual sounds and blending them into a word

Developing phonological awareness begins early. This is why reading aloud to your child at an early age is so important. Books with predictable rhyming patterns are particularly good. And don't forget nursery rhymes and rhyming songs! My 3-year-old grandson, Jack, loves to play the rhyming game in the car. We take turns coming up with silly rhymes—tickle-pickle, fat-cat. No rules—just a lot of giggles!

Formal instruction in phonological awareness typically begins in the second half of kindergarten or in first grade. Ask your child's teacher about the school's curriculum for phonological awareness and how you can support classroom instruction at home. For children with early reading difficulties, intensive instruction in phonological awareness can be especially important. If your child is having difficulty with phonological awareness beyond first grade, talk with your child's teacher to develop a strategy for the next steps.

How to help your child with letter recognition

When children first learn to read, they typically learn a few words by sight. They might learn to read their name, some words that are important to them (*mom, ice cream*), and words they see around them (*STOP, food*). Many children learn to read whole words before they can recognize and identify all the letters in the alphabet.

Recognizing words by sight without knowing the letters of the alphabet has its limitations, however. Our writing system is based on an alphabet, so eventually children need to master the basic "ingredients" of this system—letters—to become mature readers. Like many children, my daughter, Jamie, learned her letters through *Sesame Street*. The show started on television the year she was born.

Check with your child's teacher about how letters are introduced in the classroom and use your child's homework and handouts as a guide for how to help out at home. Helping your child learn the letters of his first and last name is a good place to start. Once he has these letters mastered, try introducing a few more letters and review those he has already learned.

As your child is learning his letters, make sure he understands these basic concepts:

1. Letters have names.

2. Letters represent sounds.

3. Letters can have different shapes (capital, lowercase, manuscript, cursive) but still have the same name and sound.

4. Letters make words.

When you're talking to your child about letters, remember to connect reading and writing. Help your child form letters using the same writing style that your child's teacher recommends. The handwriting charts on pages 160 and 162 can also serve as models for you. Supply crayons, markers, and other writing materials to add variety.

Some children require three-dimensional forms of letters to be able to learn and remember them. Magnetic letters or letters cut from sandpaper enable children to not only visualize but also feel the shape of each letter. Playing with blocks inscribed with letters or letters from board games such as Scrabble are other ways you can help your child learn letters. Encourage your child to make up games with these materials that you can play together.

Here are some other ideas for helping your child learn letters:

- Check out alphabet books from the library. Read them over and over again to your child. You might be surprised by the number of ABC books available today. Make a game of it—take your child to the library and see how many different alphabet books you can find.

- Create an alphabet book with your child. After you've read several alphabet books together, you and your child can write your own. Perhaps your child can think of a favorite word to put on each page, or you can create an ABC book based on a theme, such as animals or food.

- Make a dictionary with your child. Write one letter at the top of each page of a notebook, and collect words to put in your dictionary. Your child can even illustrate the words and make it a "pictionary."

- Develop letter radar. Be on alert for letters all around you—on posters, street signs, and advertisements. Make a game of it—see how many *Ms* you can find when you are on your next car trip or bus ride.

Don't restrict yourself to sitting at a table with pen and paper in hand. Find creative ways to help your child learn letters. Here are some fun ways others have tried:

- Get a large cake pan and a bag of fine sand. Pour the sand in the pan and show your child how to trace letters in it. Or do this activity in the sandbox or while at the beach; let your child trace letters in the snow or even in mud.

- Younger children like to use finger paint to practice their letters. (This can be messy, so be prepared.) You can also use chocolate pudding instead of finger paint as a special treat.

- Another alternative to paper and pencil is clay. Have your child form letters from clay or use letter-shaped cookie cutters to make letters.

- Children's books and letters in the everyday environment are the best resources for teaching your child about letters. The more "real" the materials,

the better. Give your child a stack of old magazines or catalogs, and tell him to cut out a particular letter or words starting with that letter. Make a collage of a letter, or hunt for letters in alphabet soup or cereals.

▌Resources

Letter Recognition

Alphabet City by Stephen T. Johnson (New York: Puffin, 1999). In a series of realistic pastels and watercolors, a simple sawhorse can contain the letter "A" while lampposts alongside a highway can form a row of elegant, soaring Ys. This wordless alphabet book will appeal to young and old alike.

26 Interactive Alphabet Mini-Books by Mary Beth Spann (New York: Scholastic, 1999). The eight-page mini-books for each letter of the alphabet give readers the opportunity to practice writing the letter in upper and lowercase, finding the letter in print, and seeing words and pictures of objects that begin with each letter. Children can personalize each of the mini-books.

How to help your child with phonics

"Phonics" refers to the relationships between sounds and letters. As you've probably heard, phonics instruction can be controversial. Some parents and educators insist it's the key to learning how to read. The findings of the National Reading Panel concur with this belief. However, others believe reading instruction should focus on immersing children in genuine, meaningful reading of children's books instead. They believe that teaching phonics and word recognition should be more incidental and based on individual needs.

What people *do* agree on is that letters represent sounds, and we have to know how letters and sounds relate in order to read words. Research shows that many children seem to learn this naturally and independently. Others need direct instruction and daily guided practice for several months, and some require intensive help.

The real debate over phonics revolves around not *whether* phonics should be taught but *how* it should be taught. Should phonics be taught directly using carefully sequenced workbook pages? Or should phonics be taught more naturally, using children's literature and words in the every-day environment? In either case, should phonics be taught through activities such as singing or using materials that enable children to touch and feel letters?

What can you do? At the beginning of the school year, talk to your child's teacher about how phonics is taught in the class-room and ask how you can help at home. It's also a good idea to familiarize yourself with the basic components of a sound-letter relationship curriculum.

A PHONICS PRIMER

Consonants: Twenty-one letters of the alphabet representing twenty-eight sounds. Phonics instruction includes lessons in consonants at the beginning, middle, and end of words.

Vowels: Every word has a vowel—*a, e, i, o, u,* and sometimes *y* or *w.* Phonics instruction includes lessons in both short- and long-vowel patterns.

Consonant digraphs: Two or three con-sonants next to each other that create a new sound (for example: *ch* in *child, teacher,* or *touch*).

Consonant blends: Two or three conso-nants next to each other that are blended but retain their original sound (for exam-ple: *bl* in *blow, trouble,* or *bulb*).

Diphthongs: Vowel combinations that create a complex sound (for example: *oi* in *oil, ow* in *power,* and *aw* in *claw*).

R-controlled vowels: Vowels followed by the consonant *r.* The *r* causes a shift in the pronunciation of the vowel (for example: *ar* in *art* or *car*).

Parents can help their children learn phonics by using commercially published materials and programs designed explicitly for phonics practice. However, be sure that what you do is consistent with what is being taught at school to avoid confusing your child.

C A U T I O N

You may have seen and heard enticing TV and radio ads for commercial phonics pro-grams that promise quick and miraculous results. Be aware that educators have expressed several concerns about the claims these programs make.

Figuring out words is a process that uses three systems of cues: (1) phonics, (2) meaning, and (3) grammar. Some children overuse one or more of these systems and under use the others. For example, look at the sentence "I bought a pair of boots at the shoe store." A child who reads *boats* for *boots* is paying attention to phonics, because she correctly reads the word's beginning and ending. The child is also attending to grammar, because the sentence requires a plural noun. However, the child is not attending to meaning, because you can't buy boats at a shoe store. Which cueing systems a particular child needs to work on can be determined through careful diagnosis by a reading specialist. Remember that there is no "right" way to help every child read.

- The method and sequence of commercial programs may not match instruction in your child's classroom.

- The pacing can be very rapid and may confuse children who have reading difficulties.

- There's also a danger that a program can be considered a substitute to such important practices as reading aloud.

- Finally, many of these programs focus on fluency rather than comprehension. Children may learn to "read" on their own, but they may not learn to understand the message in the writing. And understanding written messages is the primary purpose of reading.

▌Resources

Phonics

The Great Big Book of Fun Phonics Activities (Grades K–2) by Claire Daniel (New York: Scholastic, 1999). This book is a terrific collection of phonics games and other activities. It's filled with lots of ideas to add variety to phonics lessons.

Phonics They Use: Words for Reading and Spelling by Patricia M. Cunningham (Boston: Allyn & Bacon, 2004). The phonics activities are fun (tongue twisters are used for letter sound awareness, for example) and are based on solid research. Includes new chapters on fluency and assessment, new activities and strategies, an adaptable fluency development lesson, updated research grounding this approach, and a glossary of phonics jargon teachers need to know.

Teaching Phonics Today: A Primer for Educators by Dorothy S. Strickland (Newark, DE: International Reading Association, 1998). A simple, straightforward monograph on teaching phonics, written by one of the country's leading educators, this book provides a clear presentation of the phonics controversy in an easy-to-follow question and answer format.

How to help your child with word patterns

Even very young readers are good at detecting word patterns. In fact, they are usually much better at detecting word patterns than they are at learning phonics or spelling rules. Fortunately, knowledge of word patterns is an important reading skill. For example, if your child can read the word *pet,* then you can help him discover that *met* and *set* follow the same pattern. Similarly, recognizing *pet* can lead to an understanding of how to read *pen* and *peg.*

You can help your child learn basic word patterns. Did you know that 500 words can be built from the following 37 fragments? Use these patterns to make lists of rhyming words with your child. (*Examples:* back, pack, sack; bail, fail, hail, jail, mail, pail, rail, sail, tail; gain, main, pain, rain.) Your child will have more fun and learn more quickly if you use individual letters made of plastic or printed on small cards or wooden blocks that he can move around. Start with two-letter patterns and gradually add others to his repertoire.

-ack	-ay	-ip
-ail	-eat	-it
-ain	-ell	-ock
-ake	-est	-oke
-ale	-ice	-op
-ame	-ick	-ore
-an	-ide	-ot
-ank	-ight	-uck
-ap	-ill	-ug
-ash	-in	-ump
-at	-ine	-unk
-ate	-ing	
-aw	-ink	

C A U T I O N

Be careful about telling your child to "look for the little words inside the big words." This can lead to words like *prepare* turning into *prep* and *are*.

▌Resources

Word Patterns

Introducing Word Families through Literature (Greensboro, NC: Carson-Dellosa, 1994). This book provides lots of examples of children's books that include word patterns as part of the text.

Making Words by Patricia M. Cunningham and Dorothy P. Hall (Redding, CA: Good Apple, 1994). This book shows lots of ways to have fun while teaching word patterns to children in grades 1–3.

How to help your child with sight words

All children need to develop a set of words they can recognize instantly. Some English words are best learned by sight, as they have no sound-symbol regularity; common examples are *there* and *one*. Other words occur so frequently in the English language that they should be known immediately; it's not efficient to sound them out.

You can help your child develop a bank of words to recognize quickly and easily. Ask the teacher to supply you with a list of words for your child to learn by sight. This list may be derived from your child's basal reader, or it may be recommended by your school system. If the teacher can't give you a list, you may want to use one of the sample lists found on pages 146–151. Compiled by Edward Fry, these lists of words occur frequently in children's books and are well respected and widely used.

Here's how to get started with sight words training:

1. Choose three words for your child to learn.

2. Write the first word on an index card.

3. Pronounce the word.

4. Talk about what the word means.

5. Work together to come up with a sentence using the word. Write the sentence on the back of the index card.

6. Repeat steps 2–5 for the other two words.

7. At the end of the study session, review all three words.

8. At your next study time, flash the three words to your child. For each one she reads correctly, put a check mark on the index card. If she misses a word, offer encouragement, show her the sentence on the back of the card, and review the pronunciation and meaning of the word.

9. Add a few new words.

10. After a word gets five checks, enter the word into your child's personal dictionary (a notebook with one alphabet letter per page). Review the words in the dictionary from time to time.

How many words should you attempt to teach during a single sitting? That depends on your child's age, attention span, and tolerance for frustration, as well as the level of difficulty of the words you're teaching. Start with three words per homework session and increase this number gradually as time permits (and your child's interest allows). Build up to a maximum of 15–20 minutes of study per day for younger students, 30 minutes per day for older students.

Most of us have forgotten enormous amounts of information we learned as children. Information not used quickly "disappears" from our memories. That's why it's important to review anything you teach your child. Different children will, of course, require different amounts of review. Here are some general guidelines:

- For children of above-average ability, it may take 15–20 exposures to a new word before it becomes a part of their long-term vocabulary.

- For children of average or below-average ability, this may take 35–65 meaningful exposures.

Be patient—and remember that what you're doing is important to your child's reading success, which directly affects your child's school success and life success.

Using games to practice sight words and word patterns

Before too long, both you and your child will grow weary of using flash cards and lists to practice reading skills. Homemade games can add variety, spark, and enjoyment to what's basically a rote task. Here are four suggestions you can try:

1. Make Bingo, Tic-Tac-Toe, Dominoes, or board games targeting specific words. (These can be fun family projects.) For suggestions, see Chapter 10.

2. Make a double set of flash cards and play Concentration (see pages 133–134), a game in which it's easy to add new words or replace learned words. Words read correctly can be fed into a piggy bank.

3. Invent riddles. *Example:* "I'm thinking of a word that starts like *pet* and rhymes with *man*."

4. Adapt almost any card game for instructional purposes. Instead of matching numbers or suits, children can match words that rhyme *(hat, that)*, words that have the same vowel sound *(bake, aim)*, or words that have the same blend *(slow, sly)* or digraph *(child, chore)*, to name just a few. (A digraph is a group of two successive vowels—*oi, oy, ow, ou*—or consonants—*sh, ch, th, wh*—that form a single sound.)

How to help your child with longer words

By the end of third grade, most children are reading multisyllabic words. If they are to become rapid readers, they must learn to recognize frequently occurring prefixes, suffixes, and roots. This is the way most adults tackle unknown words. *Example:* An adult reading *microorganism* might recognize the prefix *micro-* as meaning "very small," the root *-organ-* as meaning "alive," and the suffix *-ism* as indicating that the word is a noun.

For fun, test yourself on the longest word in the English language (and you thought it was *antidisestablishmentarianism*):

pneumoultramicroscopic- silicovolcanoconiosis

Try to decipher this *before* checking an unabridged dictionary!

When teaching your child prefixes and suffixes, work on only a few at a time. Since it's easier to teach prefixes than suffixes (their meanings are more concrete), focus on prefixes first.

The most effective approach is to teach each prefix in the context of several words. *Example:* Teach *dis-* in *disagree, disappear,* and *disobey.*

Be sure that the words you choose are good examples of the prefix. *Example:* For teaching *in-* as the opposite of *out-, inside* is a good example while *incorrect* is not.

COMMON PREFIXES

Prefix	Meaning	Examples
bi-	two	bicycle, binoculars
dis-	not	disagree, disappear, disobey
ex-	out of	exit, expel
in-	into	inside, infiltrate
in-	not	incorrect, insincere
mis-	wrong	misspell, mistake
pre-	before	prefix, precede
post-	after	postwar, posterior
re-	again; anew	reread, rewrite
re-	back	return, retreat
sub-	under	submarine, subway
super-	above; over	superman, superior
trans-	across	transportation, transition
tri-	three	tricycle, triangle
un-	not	unhappy, untrue

Present each new word in a sentence pair that focuses on its meaning. *Example:* "I agree with you. She *disagrees* with you."

You might want to check out the following book—it provides lots of practice in using root words, prefixes, and suffixes: *Making Big Words* by Patricia M. Cunningham and Dorothy P. Hall (Redding, CA: Good Apple, 1994).

When teaching your child suffixes, it's usually enough if he learns to recognize the pronunciation of the chunks (*example:* -tion = "shun") and can tell whether the suffix indicates a noun, verb, adjective, or adverb. Only suffixes with clear meanings (*examples: -ess* = woman, *-ful* = full, *-less* = without) should be taught to elementary school children, following the suggestions given above for teaching prefixes.

For lists of word patterns, prefixes, suffixes, roots, and other reading-related lists, see *The Reading Teacher's Book of Lists,* fourth edition, by E. B. Fry, J. E. Kress, and D. L. Fountoukidis (Paramus, NJ: Prentice Hall, 2000).

COMMON SUFFIXES: NOUNS

Suffix	Examples
-al	removal, approval
-ance	clearance, importance
-ence	absence, presence
-ity	stupidity, curiosity
-ment	excitement, argument
-ness	fairness, craziness
-sion	division, explosion
-tion	multiplication, addition, subtraction

COMMON SUFFIXES: NOUNS THAT REFER TO PERSONS

Suffix	Examples
-ant	servant, giant
-ent	student, president
-er	farmer, teacher, dancer
-ess	waitress, actress
-ist	artist, cartoonist
-or	actor, sailor

COMMON SUFFIXES: VERBS

Suffix	Examples
-en	strengthen, weaken
-ify	beautify, glorify
-ize	summarize, capitalize

COMMON SUFFIXES: ADJECTIVES

Suffix	Examples
-able	movable, drinkable
-al	musical, choral
-ent	present, absent
-ful	careful, thoughtful
-ic	artistic, gigantic
-ive	creative, active
-less	careless, thoughtless
-ly	sadly, truly
-ous	curious, religious

COMMON SUFFIXES: ADVERBS

Suffix	Examples
-ally	naturally, totally
-ly	slowly, quickly

Help!

"My daughter's teacher told me that she is having trouble with phonics. A friend of mine who's an elementary school teacher gave me some materials to use at home. My daughter did just fine on these, but her grade in reading is still a D."

Phonics can be taught and tested in many different ways. The materials supplied by your friend may address phonics or other word recognition skills in ways that your daughter's reading materials at school do not. Show the materials to her teacher, ask to see your daughter's in-class work and tests, and ask your daughter's teacher to furnish you with supplementary materials to use at home.

"My third-grader is still having trouble with letter sounds and knows only a few basic words. The teacher has referred him for testing for a special program, but that could take months—maybe most of this school year. Meanwhile, he seems to be slipping farther and farther behind."

If your family doesn't have the resources for private testing and tutoring, you can still take positive action. Request a meeting with the school principal, your son's teacher, and the special education teacher or reading specialist in your son's school. Ask specifically what you can do at home to help your son with reading while you're waiting for his evaluation for a special program.

"My daughter is in fourth grade and a terrific reader. The problem is that everyone in her class—including high, medium, and low readers—all read the same novels. Frankly, I think that my daughter is being held back. The books they read are just too simple for her, and she gets bored. On the other hand, some parents I've talked to think that their children are frustrated because the novels are too hard for them. Why don't they have reading groups like when I was in school?"

There are advantages to having students of different reading levels use the same materials and learn to read in mixed-abilities groups. Classroom discussions can be more lively, lower readers can learn from higher readers (and vice versa), and teachers can provide instruction in skills to the class as a whole. You may want to ask your daughter's teacher to provide you with lists of supplementary readings—books and other materials that are related to what the class is reading but offer more challenge in terms of reading level.

"My son is in third grade. His teacher says that she teaches reading using 'balanced literacy.' What does that mean?"

The intent of balanced literacy programs is to bring the best from traditional and whole language perspectives. (While traditional instruction focuses on systematic phonics instruction and a skills-oriented approach to reading, whole language is a philosophy of teaching that integrates reading, writing, listening, and speaking and emphasizes incidental teaching of phonics and use of authentic reading materials such as trade books and magazines.) Different school systems, schools, and classroom teachers define balanced literacy differently and translate it into practice in different ways. Ask your child's teacher precisely what he or she means by balanced literacy. Also, ask the questions listed on page 34 to find out more about your son's reading program.

"My son sounds out almost every word on the page and has no idea what he is reading. What can I do?"

Your son may have been taught to read with an excessive dose of phonics. He needs to learn that this approach doesn't always work. You may want to let him record his reading on audiocassette. By reading and rereading passages into the tape recorder and listening to his tapes, he may develop greater fluency. You may also want to use flash cards with words he misses frequently to help him develop a large bank of sight words. Most important, emphasize to your son the importance of reading for meaning.

"When my daughter reads, she reverses letters. I'm afraid she might be dyslexic."

Just as Mommy is Mommy whether viewed from the front or the back, some young children see *b* as *b* even when it's facing the other way. If such reversals persist into the third grade, talk to your child's teacher. Rather than immediately suspecting the presence of dyslexia—a nebulous term used differently by different professionals—try the solutions presented on pages 63–64.

"The man who does not read good books has no advantage over the man who can't read them."

MARK TWAIN

4

How to Help Your Child with

Fluency, Vocabulary, and Reading Comprehension

How to help your child with fluency

Parents know that when their children can read with ease, they are more likely to enjoy reading and are more willing to spend time doing it. Research now confirms the importance of smooth and easy reading, called "reading fluency." Reading fluency is the bridge between word recognition and comprehension. If students take a long time to read each word, meaning can be lost.

One of the most powerful ways to help your child become a more fluent reader is through repeated readings out loud. Reading the same passage or short book many times gives children the practice they need to become better readers. You should read aloud to your child, but also give your child opportunities to read aloud to you.

10 ways to help your child read aloud

Both oral reading (reading aloud) and silent reading (reading to oneself) are important for children of any age. Schools tend to emphasize oral reading in the early grades; this helps young children concentrate and helps teachers diagnose reading difficulties. Silent reading is faster and allows children to skim, reread, or adjust their speed as necessary. Because of these factors, and because adults do far more silent reading than oral reading, the emphasis shifts as children progress through the grades.

Young children may mumble to themselves as they read "silently." As long as they need this crutch, they should not be forced to stop using it. Even adults revert back to it when they are tired or when they are reading something that requires a lot of concentration. If it becomes a bad habit for your child, the teacher can work on gradually reducing it (and you can help at home).

Naturally, you'll want to make sure to choose books that your child can actually *read*—in other words, books that aren't too difficult or advanced. A good test of suitability is to have your child read the first page silently, raising a finger each time she comes across an unknown word. If there are more than five unknown words on the first page, try to find another, simpler book on a similar topic.

You may be surprised to discover that your child can handle material that would otherwise be out of her reach—*if* the material is something of keen interest to your child, or *if* the topic is one she already knows a lot about. The more you converse with your child, the more topics she will be familiar with. The moral of this story is: You can help your child's reading immeasurably by talking to her often and at length. As a bonus, you'll also be helping to develop your child's vocabulary and fund of general information.

It's important for your child to *understand* what she is reading. The story's meaning may be lost if she has to stop too often to decode unknown words. To minimize this problem, try these strategies:

1. Scan the story to find words that may be difficult for your child to read or understand. Go over these words with her in advance.

2. Allow your child to read through a story silently before reading it aloud. (This is particularly important for children who are self-conscious about oral reading.)

3. Read a story aloud to your child before asking her to read it. (Don't be surprised if she wants to hear the same story over and over again.) This will free her from having to decode unknown words, will clarify the story structure, and *will make reading more enjoyable*—a very important benefit. Granted, this strategy may result in more memorizing than reading, but it definitely has its place. As one child says, "Reading can sure be fun when you know how!"

4. Let your child read a favorite story into a tape recorder (preferably when there is no one around to listen). Your child might also want to record stories for younger children. (This is especially great for older children reading at a low level; it avoids the stigma of reading "baby books.") Another idea is to suggest that she make a "greatest hits" cassette or CD to give to grandparents, other family members, or friends. You can even let her create a new cover for the cassette or CD with artwork or a personal photograph.

5. Have your child take turns reading parts of a story with someone else—another family member, a friend, a neighbor, a sitter, even a teddy bear.

6. Make videotapes of your child reading aloud. These become great keepsakes and also give you a way to watch your child's progress in reading over the years.

7. Read story beginnings aloud to your child to "hook" her interest; then let your child finish the story independently.

8. Add variety to reading sessions by taking turns: you read one line, she reads the next line, and so on through a story.

9. If a story includes dialogue, assume the role of one or more characters and have your child take on another. Read "in character" using different voices, accents, and inflections.

10. Keep interruptions to a minimum. Save phonics lessons for later so your child won't lose track of the story line or meaning. If she misreads several words, correct only those that affect the meaning of the story. (*Example:* It's more important to correct *can't* read as *can* than *the* read as *a*.) Make less critical corrections at a time when she misreads only a few words and comprehends well.

How to help your child with word meanings

Kids are word magnets. Estimates are that the average child knows 2,500 when entering school and 70,000 when graduating from high school. That's a lot of words.

In general, there are two types of vocabulary taught in school—general and technical. *General vocabulary* refers to words used in ongoing speaking, listening, reading, and writing. *Technical vocabulary* refers to words associated with a particular subject or area of knowledge.

Your child may have vocabulary tests on general vocabulary, vocabulary from his reading textbooks, or vocabulary from science, social studies, or other school subjects. The vocabulary curriculum can also include figurative language such as idioms (It's raining cats and dogs), metaphors (The sky is pea soup), similes (He jumped like a kangaroo), or proverbs (A stitch in time saves nine).

In general, flash cards help in preparing for vocabulary tests (word on front; meaning on back). Here are some additional tips for helping your child learn new vocabulary:

- Point out that words can have more than one meaning.

- Provide your child with opportunities to use words learned in school in other contexts.

- When helping your child study lists of vocabulary words and their meanings, work on a few words at a time. Don't try to master ten new words in a single sitting; pace the learning.

- Remember that there are different levels of learning new words. You can simply recognize the meaning (on a multiple-choice test, for example), then you can generate the meaning of the word, and, finally, you can use the word in a sentence. Try to push your child to higher levels of word learning. Keep the lists of vocabulary words that your child learns throughout the year and try to work those new words into conversations at home.

How to help your child understand and respond to stories

Have you ever heard someone say, "I'm sorry I saw the movie—the book was so much better, and the characters in the movie weren't as I imagined"? When many of us read a story, we create a "movie" in our minds. We envision the setting, identify with the characters, and respond with empathy, anger, excitement, joy, sadness, or fear. The story comes alive.

How can you make stories come alive for your child? Following are some suggestions for helping your child become personally involved with a story. This engagement not only can improve your child's understanding of the story but also can spark meaningful responses to the author's message.

Sometimes it's easier to help your child understand and respond to stories when you read them aloud. However, as your child gets older, she will begin to read independently. The following suggestions can be used whether you read along with your child or she reads on her own. A reproducible form for guiding you through this procedure can be found on pages 156–157.

1. GET READY

Before reading, think about ways to get your child involved with the story. If the story is set in a place or time that is unfamiliar to your child, bring out the atlas or encyclopedia and help her think about where and when the story takes place.

2. GET SET

After your child has read the first few pages or chapters, talk about the main character in the story. Try to get your child "involved" with the character and his or her situation. Help your child imagine what she would do if placed in a similar situation. Talk about how the character and the character's circumstances relate to her own life.

3. GO!

As your child reads the story, check in from time to time to see how the character's situation is developing, how your child is reacting to the developments, and what she predicts will happen next. Have her read aloud sections of the story she thinks are particularly meaningful. You may want to give her several bookmarks or sticky notes to mark special passages to share with you.

4. COOL DOWN

Immediately after reading the story, talk with your child about personal reactions to the story. What did she like and dislike about it? Did the story introduce moral or ethical issues that she wants or needs to discuss with you? Also talk with your child about the author's writing style.

5. FOLLOW UP

Often, when your child's teacher assigns a story, the assignment will also include activities for your child to complete before, during, or after reading. When this isn't the case, you might think about how your child can respond to the story through art, writing, drama, cooking, or perhaps by reading another book from the same genre or by the same author.

How to help your child understand informational text

Informational (expository) text is designed to teach—to provide information about a topic. Science, social studies, and health textbooks are examples of informational text. Informational textbooks are frequently loaded with new concepts, vocabulary, and facts. Often, students are required not only to read this information but also to learn it for tests, so quick, superficial reading won't do. Here are some suggestions for helping your child understand informational text:*

---

*This strategy is adapted from "Collaborative Strategic Reading" by J. K. Klingner, S. Vaughn, and J. S. Schumm. *Elementary School Journal* 99 (1998): 3–22.

1. Preview the reading assignment. Look at the pictures, the headings and subheadings, the introduction, and any summaries. Try to predict what the assignment is about.

2. Talk briefly about the topic. Ask your child what he already knows about the topic and what he expects to learn by reading the passage.

3. Break up the reading assignment into a few short sections (headings and subheadings should help).

4. Read the first section with your child—either silently or aloud, whatever seems most appropriate. Talk about words, sentences, or ideas that seemed difficult or confusing to your child (the "clunks").

5. Work together to think of ways to fix clunks.

6. Ask your child to tell you the key ideas from the section you read.

7. Read the next section. Once again, talk about clunks and key ideas.

8. After reading the whole assignment, talk about the most important ideas that your child has learned.

9. Take turns predicting questions that the teacher might ask on a test.

10. Discuss what else your child would like to learn about the topic.

This procedure takes some time, but it's worth the effort. By following these steps, your child can learn how to link new information to what he already knows, "fix up clunks," and identify the most important ideas in a passage. Remember, you're helping your child develop strategies to read and study more efficiently and effectively.

▊ Resources

Informational Text

Improving Reading: Strategies and Resources by Jerry L. Johns and Susan Davis Lenski (Dubuque, IA: Kendall/Hunt, 2001). This book is great for teaching reading skills. It provides teaching strategies, activities, and resources to help students with specific reading problems. These strategies can be adapted for emergent readers through high school. It's a practical tool that you will refer to again and again.

Questioning the Author: An Approach for Enhancing Child Engagement with Text by Isabel L. Beck, Margaret G. McKeown, Rebecca L. Hamilton, and Linda Kucan (Newark, DE: International Reading Association, 1997). This book outlines an exciting strategy, Questioning the Author, to help children become more engaged with the author's message as they read. This is a valuable resource for parents interested in promoting lively discussions with their children. The strategy can be used with either narrative or expository text.

Help!

❓ **"My daughter knows what most of the words in her social studies book say, but she doesn't comprehend well."**

This problem could be due to one or more of the following:

- Your daughter's background of vocabulary and general information may not be adequate for comprehension of the material.

- She may be paying so much attention to saying the words "right" that she has no energy left for comprehension.

- She may not understand that the purpose of reading is comprehension, not word-calling.

- She may not know how to alter her reading speed according to her purpose for reading and according to the demands of the material.

In any case, follow the steps described on pages 158–159 for reading stories or informational text.

In addition, encourage your daughter to visualize what she is reading. Because today's children watch so much TV, often they don't form the habit of making mental pictures of their own. Try one or both of these approaches:

1. Have your daughter draw pictures to illustrate what she is reading. Eventually she will be able to describe her mental pictures to you.

2. Take every opportunity to work on oral comprehension. *Example:* After watching a TV program together, ask your daughter questions like these:

- To relate the story to her own life: "Has anything like this ever happened to you?"

- To help her focus: "What were the main ideas in this program?"

- To help her recall facts from the program: "Who were the main characters?" "What did they do?" "When did the character realize that something important had happened?" "Where did this story take place?"

- To help her recognize a logical sequence: "What happened after _____ found out that _____?"

- To help her predict outcome: "What do you think will happen next?"

- To promote critical thinking: "What would have happened if _____?" "Do you agree with what happened in the story? Why or why not? Do you disagree? Why or why not?"

How to help your child follow written directions

Children (and adults) often begin a task without bothering to read the directions first. You should encourage and expect your child to read directions—as long as they are at a level your child is capable of reading. If they aren't, model reading them for your child.

When directions are complex, follow these steps:

1. Read the entire set of directions aloud, slowly and carefully.

2. Underline or circle the action(s) to be taken (the verb or verbs).

3. If the steps are not already numbered, identify and number them.

4. Help your child follow the directions.

5. Afterward, check to make sure that the directions were followed correctly.

All children need to know how to read and follow directions, and this is a skill that should be taught and reinforced early. A child who can't decipher and understand directions is a child who will have difficulty completing assignments and taking tests.

How to help your child with reading homework: A few final words

Learning to read is the key to all learning. Appalling numbers of students in the United States and Canada are functionally illiterate, unable to read job applications or simple instructions. As a caring parent, there are few responsibilities you should take as seriously as making sure that your child learns to read.

In my work, I have visited many schools and talked with teachers around the United States. I have learned how reading instruction varies tremendously from place to place. With that in mind, here's some general advice:

1. Ask questions about your child's reading program and her progress in reading.

2. Ask about specific things you can do to work with your child's teacher.

3. Take immediate steps to find more intensive help for your child if necessary.

Finally, it's important to recognize that you are the *best* person to help your child learn to understand the purpose for reading and to enjoy reading. Your own daily reading of newspapers, magazines, recipes, directions, letters, and books will demonstrate to your child the function and importance of reading. Reading aloud to your child, listening to your child read aloud, taking trips to the library, buying books and magazines as gifts, and talking about favorite books and stories are all powerful ways to share the joy of reading. The best reading homework of all is the kind of real reading you do in your home.

Help!

"My fifth grader reads stories at home to prepare for reading tests, but he fails them every time."

A casual reading of a story may not be sufficient preparation for a reading test in the middle grades. Meet with your son's teacher to inquire about the test format and find out what types of errors your son is making; it may be that the reading test is based on skills learned in class rather than mastery of the story content. If the test is story-based, you can help your son study for future tests by using the story study guides on pages 152–153 and 154–155.

"My daughter is in fifth grade. Even though she loved being read to when she was younger, now she refuses to read at all—she says it's 'boring.' I know she *can* read, because her reading test scores are great. She just *won't* read."

When children proclaim, "I don't read because it's boring," quite often it's because

they haven't found the right books! Here are some suggestions for helping your daughter find the right books:

1. Spend some time with her at the library and bookstore. Bookstores today are lively, active places—many seem more like community centers.

2. Make it a point to talk informally about books with your daughter. When she was younger, reading aloud to her was a social activity—a time for the two of you to bond. Now that she's older, sharing ideas about books you've both read, or books that you've read individually, can be a new opportunity for bonding.

3. Consider her interests. Does she like rock music, swimming, animals, sports? There are plenty of books available on all of these topics.

4. Still no "right book"? Move on to her needs. Does she want to learn how to redecorate her room, take photographs, or use email? Would she like to learn more about Colorado to help plan for a family vacation? There are tons of books available on any and all of these subjects.

5. No "right book" yet? Talk with your daughter about her favorite movie or television show. Talk with the bookstore or library staff about books focusing on related genres, topics, or story lines.

6. Don't give up! The "right book" is out there. Keep looking until you find it.

5

How to Help Your Child with
Spelling and Writing

What's new in spelling and writing instruction?

As you start helping your child with homework, you may find that significant changes have taken place in spelling and writing instruction since you were a child. Chances are that your instruction emphasized form over substance. As a result, many adults today don't write unless they absolutely have to, and even then they do it grudgingly. Following are descriptions of some differences you're likely to see—differences that may result in future adults who write well and actually *enjoy* writing.

A GREATER UNDERSTANDING OF DEVELOPMENTAL SPELLING

Much has been learned about how children progress through stages of "temporary spelling," just as they progress from crawling to walking and from babbling to understandable speech. Teachers now know that a child who spells *love* "l" has made progress from spelling it "s," and they know to nudge to gradually get "lv," "luv," and eventually "love."

A BALANCE BETWEEN FORM AND SUBSTANCE

Teachers today use a writing process in which they try to get substance out first. Then and only then do they move to expecting nice handwriting and correctness in spelling and grammar. Of course, computers greatly simplify this process! Teachers may move children from drafting to editing and polishing when there is a purpose for polishing, but not otherwise. Similarly, you will move from a draft to a final product with a letter to the editor, but not with your grocery list.

WRITING TO PROMPTS

High-stakes tests now include writing assessments in which students write to a prompt. In such tests, students generate a short essay on a specific topic that may be of several types: persuasive, expository, or narrative.

MORE STRUCTURED FEEDBACK

You probably remember getting compositions back from your teacher marked in red with lots of random comments. Teachers now use scoring guides to provide students with specific, systematic feedback about their writing.

How to help your child with spelling

Weekly spelling tests are a time-honored tradition. However, spelling programs differ from school to school and from class to class. As you prepare to help your child with spelling, find out how the program in his class is organized and run. Early in the school year, take these questions to a meeting with the teacher:

ABOUT THE ORGANIZATION OF THE PROGRAM

- "How is the class organized for spelling? As a whole class? In spelling groups? For individualized spelling?"
- "Is the program self-paced? Can each child move through spelling lessons at an individual rate?"

ABOUT YOUR CHILD'S PLACEMENT

- "Has my child been placed on, above, or below grade level in spelling?"
- "Is there any way for my child to have harder or easier spelling words, if necessary?"

ABOUT THE PROGRAM SCHEDULE

- "When are spelling words assigned or selected?"
- "When is spelling homework due?"
- "If there are spelling tests, when are they given?"

ABOUT THE FORMAT OF THE SPELLING TEST

- "Does the test consist of words only?" Or . . .
- "Does the test include other exercises, such as sentence dictation or proofreading?"

ABOUT PROGRESS REPORTS

- "How is spelling progress reported to parents?"
- "If report card grades are given in spelling, are they based on weekly spelling tests, on spelling assignments,

and/or on other assignments, such as compositions?"

Please be aware that these questions don't have right or wrong answers. They are designed to help you gather information. If there's something you don't agree with or would like to see changed, talk it over with your child's teacher.

How to help your child study spelling words

Each child learns differently, and this includes spelling words. The "ideal" number of study sessions, the "right" length of study sessions, and the "best" way to study will not be the same for every child. Experiment with your child to determine which approach works best—and be patient; it may take a while. Here are some suggestions for getting started:

SET UP A STUDY SCHEDULE

- On the day spelling words are assigned or selected, test your child on these words. Determine which ones she already knows and which ones she needs to study. For the latter, determine which *parts* of the words she already knows.

- Budget study time for the number of days allotted. Set aside time to practice new words and time to review previously mastered words.

- Limit spelling study sessions to 15–20 minutes each. Several shorter daily sessions are more productive than a night-before-the-test marathon cram session. Brief practices can be squeezed into spare moments: while driving to soccer, while waiting in the doctor's office, and so on.

- Plan a review of all words the night before the test.

DETERMINE THE WAY (OR WAYS) YOUR CHILD LEARNS BEST

Mix and match the following teaching methods:

- Have your child write each word 5, 10, or 15 times. (This works best if she writes *all* the words one time, then *all* the words a second time, and so on.)

- Have your child type words on a computer and check herself with a spellchecker program. Playing with fonts and sizes can add an extra dimension of fun!

- Write each word in large letters for your child. Then have her trace each one with a finger and pronounce it while tracing. Repeat until she can write the word from memory.

- Dictate each word to your child and have her write it down. Then have her correct the paper. This encourages closer attention to mistakes.

- Say the words into a tape recorder. Leave enough "lag time" after each so your child can write the word. This will permit repeated practices—as many as necessary, and as many as she wants— with minimal parental involvement.

- New writing techniques can make spelling fun. Writing with a finger in shaving cream on a desk or back car window can have the added benefit of a clean surface once the session is over! Favorite color crayons and markers are other possibilities.

- Spelling can also be taught through the use of games. See Chapter 10 for suggestions.

Help!

"My daughter is in fifth grade. She refuses to study for spelling tests. She says she doesn't need to learn how to spell because our computer has a spellchecker. How can I encourage her to study for her tests?"

First of all, studying for tests should not be negotiable. If your daughter needs a rationale for why learning to spell is important, explain that learning to be a better speller will help her become a better reader and writer. Particularly in the upper grades, students learn syllable analysis as well as root words, prefixes, and suffixes. This systematic study can assist with vocabulary learning as well. Work on ways to help make spelling study sessions lively, fun, and motivational.

"I work with my son on spelling words for at least an hour every Thursday night for the test on Friday. Yet he still fails his spelling tests! Our study sessions are tiring, tension-producing, and obviously nonproductive."

The following sample schedule may help improve your son's productivity and make the study experience more enjoyable for both of you. Remember to keep study sessions short—no more than 15–20 minutes.

SAMPLE SPELLING STUDY SCHEDULE

Monday

1. Pretest on the whole list, noting correct and incorrect parts of words not yet mastered.

2. Teach the first ⅓ of the words missed on the pretest.

3. Test on all words learned so far.

Tuesday

1. Test on all words learned to date.

2. Teach the second ⅓ of words missed on Monday's pretest.

3. Test on all words learned so far.

Wednesday

1. Test on all words learned to date.

2. Teach the third ⅓ of words missed on Monday's pretest.

3. Test on all words learned so far.

Thursday

1. Test on all words learned to date.

2. Practice the most difficult words.

3. Test again.

Friday

Send your child off to school with these words: "We practiced for your spelling test all week. We know you're prepared. Do the best you can today, and however you do will be fine with me."

"Every Monday, my daughter's teacher writes the week's spelling words on the board. Every Monday afternoon, my daughter comes home with a list of misspelled words to study. We never know what to study because she doesn't have a spelling book."

Meet with the teacher to determine the root of your daughter's problem. She may have difficulty copying from the board, and she may need her vision checked. Or she may be perfectly capable of copying the words but isn't taking the time to do so.

"Every week, I give my son his spelling words and he spells them out loud to me, but then he fails his weekly spelling test. How can he know the words so well and still not pass the tests?"

Practicing spelling words orally is only one way to learn them, and it may not be the best way for your son. Try some of the other strategies outlined on pages 61–62. Make sure that your son practices *writing* the words, not just saying them.

"My daughter gets 100 percent right on every spelling test. Do I really need to help her study each week?"

It may be sufficient to pretest her on the day spelling words are assigned and let her work independently from there. If she continues to ace the tests, however, you may want to schedule a conference with the teacher to find out why. Possible reasons include:

- The spelling list words may not be challenging enough for your daughter. She may need to be moved to a higher

spelling group or be given a list of supplemental challenge words to work on.

- The words may be of an appropriate level of difficulty, but the teacher may provide enough in-class drill that practice at home is not necessary.

How to help your child with handwriting

Helping your child with handwriting takes patience, patience, and more patience. Many children don't like the process of writing by hand. (Many adults don't, either. Why else are computers so popular?) I know one young boy who will gladly spend hours making elaborate drawings of buildings, cars, airplanes, and other complicated subjects, yet the moment he's asked to write a sentence he wails, "I *can't!* It's *too hard!*" Nevertheless, all children must master these skills to some degree. With firm and caring assistance, even the most reluctant writer will eventually come around!

WHEN TO WORRY ABOUT LETTER REVERSALS

Among reading professionals, a great deal of controversy exists around the topic of letter and word reversals. For example, many experts maintain that reversals are not the *cause* of learning problems but a *symptom.* They disagree among themselves about the best way to approach this issue and which remedial tactics are most effective. Naturally, this controversy has led to widespread confusion among parents.

All children who make reversals do not "have dyslexia," any more than all thin children have anorexia nervosa. Before concluding that your child has learning problems, consider the following:

- Reversals are quite common among children in the early years of grade school. They usually begin to subside by age 8 or 9.

- Reversals of the letters *b* and *d* can sometimes be eliminated through this simple trick: Have the child make two fists with thumbs stuck up to form a "bed." The *b* in the word *bed* is its head (left hand); the *d* is its foot (right hand). (Since most children write on their hands anyway, go ahead and give your child permission to do it this time. The lesson will be even more unforgettable.)

- If the problem persists, or if the reversals are coupled with other obvious learning difficulties, consider having your child professionally evaluated. Ask the teacher about the school's procedures or seek outside testing.

How to improve your child's printing

Many children have difficulty learning to print. If this seems to be true for your child, it may be due to one or more of the following reasons:

- The teacher isn't allowing enough in-class practice time.

- Your child isn't interested in writing.

- Your child doesn't realize that legible writing is an important means of communication.

- Your child's fine motor coordination may be developing more slowly than that of other children in the class.

There are many ways to help your child improve his printing skills. Experiment with the techniques that follow, or ask the teacher for additional suggestions. See page 160 for a chart showing the traditional Zaner-Bloser style of printing; you may want to copy and use this chart for practice sessions at home. *Important:* Check with the teacher first to make sure that the Zaner-Bloser style is the one your child is learning in school. If the teacher is using another style, ask for a manuscript chart you can use at home. Also make sure that your sequence or pacing of instruction does not conflict with the teacher's plan for the year.

- Allow 10–15 minutes per night, four nights per week for printing practice.

- Teach four letters per week for 13 weeks. Start with the lowercase letters; then move on to the capital letters.

Once your child has learned a few letters, use the following routine to ready him for forming words:

1. During each week's first practice session, have your child practice the four letters of the week on manuscript practice paper. See page 161 for a sample you can copy and give to your child.

2. During each week's second practice session, have your child practice the letters again and focus on letters that were most challenging.

3. During each week's third practice session, have your child practice the letters in real words on manuscript practice paper. Assign words that position the new letter at the beginning, the middle, and the end. *Examples:* see, mu_s_t, pet_s_.

4. During each week's final practice session, have your child review all letters learned to date. For this practice, he should use regular writing paper rather than manuscript practice paper.

Keep practice sessions brief and fun. Let your child use colored pencils, crayons, and various other writing instruments for further motivation.

Following each practice session, have your child examine his writing and identify ways it can be improved. The "3S" method is one way to approach this. Your child asks herself these questions about each letter:

- "Is the letter the right *Size*?"
- "Is the letter the right *Shape*?"
- "Did I leave enough *Space* between letters and words?"

Encourage your child to write by posting practice pages on the refrigerator or sending them to grandparents or other admiring adults.

How to improve your child's cursive writing

Many children have difficulty making the transition from printing (manuscript) writing to cursive (script) writing. If this seems to be true for your child, it may be due to one or more of the following reasons:

- The teacher isn't allowing enough in-class learning and practice time.
- Your child may have problems writing individual letters.
- Your child may be able to write the letters correctly but has problems connecting them.
- Comments from the teacher may be so general (*example:* "Your handwriting is messy") that they give no real direction for improvement.
- Your child may not like to write, and as a result may be hasty and careless with letter and word formation.

Most intermediate students can substantially improve their formation and connection of cursive letters with regular, systematic, intensive practice. And once they learn to write correctly, their speed and attitude improve.

Children should be allowed to write in whichever way is most comfortable for them—printing or cursive—after they have learned both modes. Children should also be taught to use a computer keyboard if all else fails. Following are several suggestions for helping your child master cursive. See pages 162–165 for a Zaner-Bloser cursive chart, a practice sample, and practice paper you can copy and use at home. (Again, check with the teacher first to make sure that Zaner-Bloser is the style your child is learning in school.)

Practice paper is especially effective in motivating children to develop a uniform size and slant for their cursive letters. Colored felt-tipped pens or markers make it fun and easy because they literally glide across the page.

One more tip before you begin: Cursive practice is more than an intellectual learning process; it's also a *physical* learning process. The hand, wrist, arm, elbow, and shoulder must be taught specific patterns of movement. The more your child practices, the more habitual these patterns will become. (In a way, learning to write cursive is a lot like learning to ride a bicycle.)

- Allow 10–15 minutes per night, four nights per week for cursive practice.

- Teach four letters per week for 13 weeks. Start with the lowercase letters; then move on to the capital letters.

1. During each week's first practice session, have your child practice the four letters of the week on cursive practice paper. See page 165 for a sample you can copy and give to your child.

2. During each week's second practice session, have your child practice the letters again and focus on letters that were most challenging.

3. During each week's third practice session, have your child practice the letters in real words on cursive practice paper. Assign words that position the new letter at the beginning, the middle, and the end. *Examples:* book, able, sob.

4. During each week's final practice session, have your child review all letters learned to date. For this practice, she should use regular writing paper rather than cursive practice paper.

Keep practice sessions brief and fun. Let your child use colored pencils, crayons, and various other writing instruments for further motivation.

Following each practice session, have your child examine her writing and identify ways it can be improved. The "4S" method is one way to approach this. Your child asks herself these questions about each letter:

- "Is the letter the right **S**ize?"

- "Is the letter the right **S**hape?"

- "Are all the letters **S**lanted in the same direction and at the same angle?"

- "Did I leave enough **S**pace between letters and words?"

Supplement practice sessions with opportunities for "real" writing. Invite your child to help you prepare party invitations, shopping lists, and thank-you notes. Encourage her to write letters to grandparents or friends.

Help!

"My daughter's handwriting is awful! Her papers were just fine when she was in second grade last year.

But now that she is in third grade and has to use cursive, her teacher is constantly writing negative comments on her papers.**"**

Talk with the teacher to discover the source of your daughter's problem. Cursive is usually introduced in the third grade, so the teacher is right on schedule. Your daughter may need more practice than other children in her class. Make regular practice sessions a part of her daily homework schedule.

"My son knows how to make all of his cursive letters, yet his papers are still a mess. He refuses to slow down and write neatly."

Your son needs to understand that legible writing is a form of good manners. When our writing is messy, we're implying that we don't care whether someone else can read it or not. Also, many people judge others by their written work. Tidy, readable writing makes a good first impression that lasts.

Try letting your son use a stopwatch or a kitchen timer during his practice sessions. Encourage him to work quickly but neatly. Emphasize that it's possible to write rapidly in cursive while maintaining legibility.

"I really don't understand why my son's teacher emphasizes handwriting instruction. Shouldn't time spent on handwriting be spent on teaching students to learn to keyboard instead?"

Although "paperless classrooms" do exist, most students need to write out at least some of their work by hand. Work that is sloppy or hard for a teacher to read can result in lower grades. Moreover, many state reading and writing high-stakes tests now include open-ended questions that

students must respond to in writing. Legible handwriting continues to be important for students and adults.

How to raise your child's grades in English

The English curriculum (also known as "language" or "language arts") may include language mechanics, handwriting, spelling, and composition. It varies greatly from school to school and from text to text. As a result, there are no blanket remedies for children who experience difficulty in this area.

If your child is earning low grades in English, schedule a conference with the teacher. Let the teacher know that you want to help your child, and ask for suggestions and recommendations. Inquire about state minimum requirements and skills that must be mastered for standardized tests (often called "benchmarks"). "How to improve your child's composition" on pages 68–70 includes many suggestions you should find helpful as you work with your child.

Help!

"My son has not passed a single English test this year! He never seems to know when tests are scheduled, and he never brings his book home to study. How can I possibly help him?"

Most English books don't conform to the same neat "one-lesson-a-week, test-every-Friday" format as spelling texts. Some lessons may last for less than a week; others may take up to two weeks or more of class time. Find out from your son's teacher how lessons are set up in the text and when tests are scheduled. Ask for extra practice activities and materials your son can complete at home prior to the tests.

? **"My daughter usually performs well in language arts, but she has real trouble with punctuation. She failed the last three tests and will probably get a C this semester. Should I just forget about this problem and assume that her grade will improve as soon as the class moves on to a new unit?"**

Even though your daughter's overall grade may be respectable, it's never a good idea to "skip over" an entire set of skills. Knowing how to punctuate is essential, and if she doesn't learn it now, she will have to learn it later. (Punctuation skills are often included on standardized tests.) Ask the teacher for extra practice activities and materials your daughter can complete at home. Also find out which punctuation skills are included on standardized tests your daughter will take this year; at the very least, she should master these.

? **"My son is a whiz in English. His grades have been top-notch all year. But he never brings his book home, so I don't know what he's studying. How can I be sure that he's learning all the skills he needs to score well on our state's standardized test?"**

Talk to the teacher or the academic adviser at your school. Find out how the classroom curriculum correlates with your state's standardized test. Most schools are very conscious of state requirements and have

planned their lessons to promote success on standardized tests. A conference should provide you with the information you need to feel comfortable about this.

How to improve your child's composition

Perhaps the most important qualification you can bring to this task is . . . patience. Often children (and adults) are eager to complete a written task and are satisfied with just one draft. If children can learn the value of the prewriting-writing-revising process at an early age, their writing will be greatly improved for now and in the future. Here's a good way to break down the process into steps:

1. BRAINSTORM

Before actually beginning a composition, your child should be encouraged to *brainstorm*—to generate and list ideas. You can participate, too, as long as you play equal roles. In other words, a brainstorming session is not the time to exercise your parental authority or to insist that your ideas are the "right" ones.

Brainstorming is used in classrooms, companies, and businesses to promote creative thinking and problem solving. Fun for all, it has only three simple rules:

- Everyone tries to dream up as many ideas as possible—from serious to outrageous and everything in between.

- Any idea is considered acceptable during the brainstorming session. (Save the weeding out for later.)

- No one is allowed to criticize anyone else's ideas.

The more ideas are generated, the more successful the session will be. If your child's writing skills are not at the point where he can write quickly, then you should assume responsibility for listing the ideas as they're spoken.

What kinds of ideas can help with a composition assignment? For example, if your child's assignment is to "describe your favorite person," he can brainstorm characteristics of the person chosen and reasons why that person is worth writing about.

2. ORGANIZE

Once enough ideas have been generated, your child should organize them in a logical order. A formal outline may not be necessary, but an effort should be made to arrange the details in some kind of sequence.

3. WRITE THE FIRST DRAFT

After the general sequence has been determined, your child should write a *rough* first draft. Remind your child that now is not the time to worry about the fine points of spelling or punctuation; the purpose of the first draft is to get something (anything!) down on the page.

4. REVISE

Revisions not only take patience; they also require attention to detail. It's hard at first for young writers to revise their own work because they have not yet internalized grammar rules, and they may not see their own spelling mistakes.

The "A-OK" method is one way to make revising easier and more efficient. It directs the child to focus on one aspect of the composition at a time. Introduce it by modeling—taking your child through each step and showing how it's done. Eventually he should be able to handle it independently.

A-OK has five steps: "MOK," "POK," "SOK," "WOK," and "NOK." Each step contains two or more questions for your child to ask. How much revising is necessary depends on how your child answers the questions.

A-OK*

I. MOK ("**M**eaning **OK**")

- "Does it make sense?"
- "Are my facts correct?"
- "Did I say what I really wanted to say?"

II. POK ("**P**aragraph **OK**")

- "Is it indented?"
- "Is it made up of sentences related to *one* main idea?"
- "Is it connected logically with paragraphs that come before and after?"

III. SOK ("**S**entence **OK**")

- "Does it start with a capital letter?"
- "Does it end with the correct punctuation mark?"
- "Does it express a complete thought?"

IV. WOK ("**W**ord **OK**")

- "Is it spelled correctly?"
- "Is it capitalized correctly (if it needs to be)?"

---

*Adapted from "A-OK: A Reading for Revision Strategy" by Jeanne Shay Schumm in *Reading: Exploration and Discovery*, vol. 10, no. 1 (Fall 1987).

- "Is it the *very best* word, or is there another, better word I could use in its place?"

V. NOK ("**N**eatness **OK**")

- "Is it easy to read?"

- "Does it follow the format required by my teacher?" (Typed or handwritten? Written on every other line or double spaced? Written on one side of the paper only?)

Revising is one step of the writing process that is greatly simplified with a computer. Children who are reluctant to revise handwritten papers may be much more willing to make changes when each revision doesn't involve a complete rewrite. With the freedom a computer provides, and the extra work it saves, even children who don't like to write turn out better papers. For more information on using a computer, see Chapter 9.

One final note: Whenever possible, reading for revisions should be done out loud. Errors are easier to catch when they are said and heard than when they are read silently.

Help!

❓ "My son's stories seem more like lists of words than paragraphs. There's no capitalization or punctuation. Tyrone is in fourth grade; shouldn't his composition skills be better than this?"

Your son could benefit from regular writing practice. Start by giving him short but interesting things to write—postcards to friends or relatives, invitations, descriptions of his favorite TV shows, and so on.

Begin working on the sentence level. Show your son that each sentence begins with a capital letter and ends with a punctuation mark. After he writes a sentence, have him read it out loud and revise it using the appropriate steps of the A-OK method.

As he becomes more comfortable with his writing, encourage him to move on to longer, more sophisticated sentences. Demonstrate with a basic sentence; then slowly add and edit words to embellish it. *Example:*

"I saw a girl."

"I saw a <u>little</u> girl."

"I saw a <u>happy little</u> girl."

"I <u>noticed</u> a happy little girl <u>wearing red overalls</u>."

"I noticed a happy little girl wearing red overalls <u>and skating backwards down the sidewalk</u>."

Once your son feels confident about "SOKing" and "WOKing" sentences, he'll be ready to progress to the paragraph level and from there to more complex compositions.

❓ "My daughter is in fifth grade. She keeps talking about rubrics. What is a rubric anyway?"

Remember when you were in school and you would get a graded composition back from your teacher? Many times your paper would be covered with red ink, with your teacher's praise and suggestions for improvement. Today many teachers use a different method of responding to students' writing. They use scoring guides, or "rubrics," to give more structured feedback to students in terms of form, content, and style. Ask

SAMPLE RUBRIC

	Tip Top (4 points)	**Pretty Good** (3 points)	**Getting There** (2 points)	**Keep Working** (1 point)
Meaning	Message clear, easy to follow	Message mostly clear and easy to follow	Message somewhat clear or easy to follow	Message not clear, hard to follow
Paragraphs	Indented, has a main idea, and connects with paragraphs before and after	Mostly indented, has a main idea, and connects with paragraphs before and after	Mostly indented, has a main idea, or connects with paragraphs before and after	Not indented, has no main idea, and does not connect with paragraphs before and after
Sentences	Expresses complete thoughts and uses correct punctuation	Mostly expresses complete thoughts and uses correct punctuation	Mostly expresses complete thoughts or uses correct punctuation	Does not express complete thoughts and does not use correct punctuation
Words	Spelling correct, capitalization correct, and uses variety of words	Spelling mostly correct, capitalization mostly correct, and/or some use of a variety of words	Spelling needs correction, capitalization needs correction, or needs more use of varied words	Spelling needs correction, capitalization needs correction, and needs more use of varied words
Neatness	Easy to read and follows directions for format	Mostly easy to read and follows directions for format	Mostly easy to read or follows directions for format	Hard to read and does not follow directions for format

your daughter's teacher for a copy of the rubric he or she uses so you can see what your daughter is expected to do when writing compositions.

❓ **"My son writes interesting compositions and stories for school, but his grades are never very good because his spelling is poor. I can't figure out why he misspells words in compositions that he has spelled correctly on spelling tests."**

Chances are your son's imagination is working faster than his pencil. He's concerned with ideas over form. Congratulate him on his creativity, and let it continue to run free—on the first draft. Then insist that he use the A-OK method to revise his paper before he hands it in for a grade. (You may need to go through these steps with him several times before he can work through them by himself.) Meanwhile, have him keep a list of his misspelled words. He will become aware of which words he is missing, and you can take this opportunity to help him to learn to spell them correctly. Look back at pages 61–63 for suggestions.

If your son consistently has problems spelling while writing, consider adding this book to the reference library in his study center: the *Pocket Bad Speller's Dictionary* by Joseph Krevisky and Jordan L. Linfield (New York: Random House, 1997).

? **"My daughter always receives high grades on her compositions. She seems to have a real talent for writing. What can I do to encourage her?"**

You can introduce her to ways she might win prizes for her writing or get published. Many civic organizations sponsor writing competitions; check with the teacher, media specialist, or children's librarian. Many publications, local and national, provide space in their issues for children's writing (and some are entirely child-written). A list of publications follows.

If your daughter seems interested in submitting her work for publication, take her to the library for an afternoon of exploring those magazines the library subscribes to. To see copies of the others, write to the publishers and request samples. (You may be charged a small fee.) Help your daughter examine these thoroughly to determine what kinds of writing get published. Then let her decide if she wants to give it a try. Bolster her confidence when and if she receives rejection notices—and tell her to keep trying.

You can also encourage her to share her writing with family and friends. For example, she could make books of her short stories or poems and give them as gifts on special occasions.

▌Resources

Publications and Publishers That Accept Works by Young Writers

Boys' Life "Think & Grin." Boy Scouts of America • P.O. Box 152079 • Irving, TX 75015 • *www.boyslife.org*. Ages 6 to 18. *Boys' Life* will publish jokes written on postcards or submitted via their Web site.

Children's Better Health Institute. 1100 Waterway Boulevard • Indianapolis, IN 46202 • *www.cbhi.org/cbhi/magazines*. They will publish short stories (1,000 words), poetry, jokes, and art. Check out their Web site for more information about their seven magazines geared for ages 2 to 12.

Cricket Magazine Group. Carus Publishing Company • P.O. Box 9307 • LaSalle, IL 61301 • *www.cricketmag.com*. Cricket Magazine Group accepts pictures, stories, and poems by young readers for *Cricket* magazine's Cricket League, *Spider* magazine's Spider's Corner contest entries, and *Cicada* magazine. The specific theme and rules for each contest are found on the Submissions page at their Web site.

New Moon: The Magazine for Girls and Their Dreams • 34 East Superior Street, Suite 200 • Duluth, MN 55802 • *www.new moon.org*. This ad-free, multi-cultural magazine for girls ages 8 to 14 will publish letters, news about girls and women, "herstory" articles about girls and women from the past, articles about girls and women of today doing great things, letters about unfair things that happen to girls just because they're girls, reviews, poetry, drawings, quotes, and more. Check out their submission guidelines online.

Skipping Stones • P.O. Box 3939 • Eugene, OR 97403 • *www.skippingstones.org.* An international multicultural children's magazine for ages 8 to 16 that encourages an understanding of different cultures and languages, with an emphasis on ecology and human relationships. It includes artwork, writings, riddles, book reviews, news items, and a pen pal section; accepts work by children from around the world.

Stone Soup • P.O. Box 83 • Santa Cruz, CA 95063 • *www.stonesoup.com.* "The magazine by young writers and artists" publishes stories, poems, book reviews, and art by children and adolescents up to age 13.

*"What we have to learn to do,
we learn by doing."*

ARISTOTLE

How to Help Your Child with
Math

What's new in math instruction?

You might also ask, "Where were the calculators when I was in grade school?" And you might observe, "Math class sure has changed!" It's true: mathematics instruction has been in a state of flux for several years. Why? First of all, technology is changing. The wide availability of calculators and computers today has diminished the need for human beings to do low-level calculations. Second, job demands are more often related to higher-level thinking and decision-making than low-level calculations.

The National Council of Teachers of Mathematics (NCTM) *(www.nctm.org)* has played a strong leadership role throughout this process. In 2000, NCTM adopted six new principles to guide the planning of school mathematics programs and ten standards to serve as a framework for K–12 curricular planning. Like previous standards, the revised principles and standards put an emphasis on logical reasoning and understanding of math concepts—particularly as they relate to real-world problems—while reinforcing the need for basic computational skills.

What does a math class look like today? Chances are your child will still learn how to do basic calculations but will also receive instruction about how to develop "calculation fluency." Math classrooms today also focus on problem solving, communication, reasoning, and using mathematics with technology and other real-world applications. Also, elementary curriculums are now likely to include areas previously taught only in high school, such as basic algebra. Your child won't use just a pencil and paper for mathematics; she will also use a computer, a calculator, and lots of hands-on manipulative materials.

Because the nature of mathematics instruction has changed so radically since we adults were students, you'll want to become familiar with the curriculum and teaching procedures at your child's school. Here are some questions to guide your discussion with the teacher:

- "Please tell me about the math curriculum. In what ways is my child learning about calculation, problem solving, communication, reasoning, and connecting math to the real world?"

- "How are students grouped for math instruction?"

- "How are computers and calculators used in the classroom?"

- "How is my child's progress in math monitored?"

- "How will I be informed if my child is falling behind in math?"

- "How can I support the math program at home?"

Help!

"My son is in third grade. At the beginning of the school year, we received a list of school supplies we needed to buy. A calculator was on the list. I'm worried that my son won't learn his math facts."

In the past, so much attention was placed on computation that there was insufficient time left over for learning math skills such as solving word problems and using mathematics to solve real-world problems. NCTM emphasizes the importance of developing fluency in calculation. The organization also recommends that students learn to use technology—including calculators. Ask your child's teacher how calculation and technology skills are balanced in the curriculum.

"My daughter keeps talking about 'estimating' answers. What's wrong with getting the *right* answers? I don't understand the emphasis on estimation."

In everyday mathematics, there are times when we need an exact answer and times when an approximate answer will do. When you're at the store, in the workplace, or in a discussion with a family member, you may need to do some speedy mental arithmetic to make a decision or respond to a question or an observation. *Examples:* "There's 20 percent more in the bottle, and it costs a dollar more. . . . Is it a bargain?" "Do I really agree with the proposal for the new retirement plan?" "Let's see; two dollars more allowance per week equals how much more per year?"

Knowing how to estimate is a real-life, real-world skill. Also, children who are good at estimating are able to quickly realize when an answer is way off base and rule out some incorrect choices on standardized achievement tests. If exact answers are needed, they can use calculators or pencil and paper.

Rest assured that your daughter is learning and *will* learn how to arrive at exact answers to problems. She's probably learning multiple ways to solve problems for different purposes. Talk to the teacher to find out how estimating and mental arithmetic fit into the curriculum.

? **"Math was and is my worst subject! My palms still sweat when I think about math tests, and now it's the same for my daughter. She's a basket case on test days. How can I help her?"**

Math anxiety is very real. Children and adults with math anxiety become extremely fearful of mathematics and avoid it as much as possible. Talk with your daughter's teacher and, if necessary, the school counselor. Enlist their help. Try to understand the math program at your daughter's school and be supportive of it. Avoid communicating your dislike of mathematics; instead model a positive attitude about the subject and stress the importance of math in daily life. You might compile a mental list of real-life, everyday situations where you use math. Math becomes less scary when we realize it is just a tool to help us make decisions and solve real-life problems. Also point out any instances you observe where your daughter uses math without anxiety. *Examples:* Figuring out if she has enough money to pay for a movie and popcorn; deciding whether her bed will fit in a corner or be too big; planning the time she'll need to complete a long-term project or report.

How to help your child with math concepts

Like math facts, math concepts should be taught in logical sequences. Start by familiarizing yourself with your child's math text so you can understand its sequence of instruction. Check with the teacher to find out if the materials will be taught in a different sequence or will be supplemented with others. The more informed you are, the more you will be able to help your child.

ADDITION, SUBTRACTION, MULTIPLICATION, DIVISION, DECIMALS, AND FRACTIONS

Any learning is easier with concrete aids. Start with body parts (like fingers and toes), follow with other concrete objects (like pennies and buttons), and end up with abstract numbers, and you'll have made these basic concepts much more accessible to your child.

Children need to understand that addition and subtraction are opposite operations, as are multiplication and division. They also need to understand that multiplication is a fast way of adding and that division is a fast way of subtracting. Proving answers by performing opposite operations can help bring home these concepts.

The concept of decimals is best taught with money. Using coins and bills to indicate the difference between $0.50, $5.00, and $50.00 can make lightbulbs go on over children's heads. Once children have learned decimals with money, it's easy for them to understand decimals overall.

Fractions can be more difficult to grasp. A child may quite reasonably wonder how ⅕ can be smaller than ¼, since five is more than four. Or, when one of three parts of a circle is colored in, why is this part ⅓ instead of ½, since one part is colored in and two parts aren't? Use concrete aids— slices of cake, measuring spoons, rulers, fraction puzzle pieces—to help your child "see" these concepts.

MONEY

Money concepts can be taught in a variety of ways at home. Children especially enjoy having and using their own money in practice sessions and games—as long as you promise to give it all back at the end! Here are some ideas to try with your child:

- Give your child an allowance and have him open a savings account.

- Play *Monopoly*—a great favorite among even young children. As their grasp of basic math concepts improves, they can be allowed to act as the banker.

- Practice making change. Start by teaching your child to "count up" from the cost of the item being purchased (at a real store or a "pretend store"). Children should learn to count up to coin amounts first, then to single dollars, and finally to multiple-dollar bills. Try the following tips for teaching these skills:
  - If the cost ends in a number other than 5 or 0, use pennies until you reach a number that ends with 5 or 0.

  - If the cost ends in 5 or 0, use nickels and dimes until you reach 25, 50, or 75.

  - If the cost ends in 25, 50, or 75, use quarters until you reach 100 (one dollar).

You can also use money to begin teaching an older child about percentages. Toys are usually taxed. Help your child figure out the actual cost of a toy he wants to buy by estimating the tax that will be added at the checkout counter. *Example:* "The game you want costs $4.75. The tax is 5 percent— that's 5 cents added to every dollar. $4.75 is almost $5.00. Five dollars times 5 cents equals 25 cents. Now add that to $4.75. The real price of your game will be just about $5.00."

TIME

Children naturally develop a sense of time as they grow. Young children initially perceive no difference between a week and a year. (The day following one birthday, they're likely to ask how soon they can expect the next.) This is one reason why children have so little patience when it comes to waiting for anticipated events. Anything more distant than tomorrow seems impossibly far away. Here are some ideas to help your child understand the concept of time:

- Have your child mark off days on a calendar. He will gradually come to understand how much time a week takes, and that's a step in the direction of comprehending the length of a month and even a year.

- Be sure to have at least one nondigital (analog) clock in the house. If your clock has a second hand, that's even better. The movement of a second hand is something a child can see.

- Buy your child a toy clock or a nondigital watch; then teach him to tell time in the following sequence: hour, half-hour, quarter-hour, and finally five- and then one-minute intervals. Gradually introduce the different terms for the same concepts: "three thirty" (easier) and "half past three" (harder), "four forty-five" (easier) and "a quarter to five" (harder). Pay special attention to troublesome areas. For example, children have a tendency to read 7:50 as 8:50 because the hour hand is closer to the 8 than the 7.

GEOMETRY AND MEASUREMENT

Again, use concrete aids. To a child, seeing is believing, and touching is even more convincing. Here are some ideas for home:

- Have your child build a birdhouse or other object that requires accurate measurement and may also necessitate an understanding of perimeter, area, and other concepts.

- Let your child plot his growth on a wall chart (or make pencil marks along a door jamb).

- Invite your child to help you make cookies. He can read the recipe, assist with measuring out ingredients, read the marks on the butter wrapper, and lick the spoon.

The possibilities for hands-on learning of math concepts are endless: have your child read his weight on a scale, give your child responsibility for reading the temperature on the thermometer each morning before school (and dressing accordingly), let him use tools (with supervision), and so on. Draw on your own imagination and the tasks of your daily life, as well as your hobbies, to come up with others that will interest your child.

Incidentally, it's a very good idea to teach metric along with English measures (English measures being the ones people in the United States normally use: foot, inch, ounce, pound, and so on). The metric system is the standard in most countries, and while an effort to educate the American public (through road signs showing both miles and kilometers, for example) has largely been ignored, your child will probably need to know both.

How to help your child with word problems

The purpose of most word problems is to apply math concepts to real-life situations. Many children are intimidated by these problems, as they have a hard time puzzling through the prose to find the numbers they need. The "SIR RIGHT" method can help, although some steps will be unnecessary for some problems. Teach it by modeling it for your child with one or more homework problems.

Start by reading the problem silently to get a general understanding of it.

Identify all numbers written as digits or words. It may be necessary to look for "hidden" numbers ("dozen," "half as many," and so on).

Read the problem again, this time out loud, and draw a picture or diagram of it. (Some children may be able to do this in their heads.)

Read the problem yet again to find out what it is asking for. The answer may involve working backward from the question. (As many children have discovered, it's easier to solve a maze by starting at the finish.)

Inquire, "What do I have to do to answer the problem?" Remember to add or multiply if a larger number is expected, or to subtract or divide if a smaller number is expected. Look for key words that tell you which operation is correct. *Examples:*

- "Total," "in all," and "altogether" indicate the need for addition or multiplication.
- "How much is left," "how many are left," "how many more/greater/less than," and "how much older than" indicate the need for subtraction.
- "How much . . . each" and "how many . . . each" indicate the need for division.

Give the problem smaller numbers than the ones actually used in it. If you are still puzzled by the problem, repeat the Read and Inquire steps.

Ham it up, acting out the problem if necessary.

Take a pencil and solve the problem, check your computation, and make sure that the answer makes sense.

Of course, you can also use real-life situations to make word problems more attractive to your child. Instead of asking, "If Johnny has two bananas and four friends to share them with, what should he do?" give your child two bananas the next time four friends come over and have her figure it out.

Finally, have your child make up word problems that are personally interesting to her. Problems about Harry Potter, trading cards, TV or movie stars, or hobbies are sure to be more fascinating than the ones in the math book. Research has shown that this practice helps students solve word problems on standardized tests.

Help!

"My son just cannot solve word problems. Other than that, his math homework is fine. He can read the problems, but if more than one computation process is required, he's lost."

Teach him the "SIR RIGHT" method explained on pages 79–80. Work through it with him until he is able to act independently.

"My daughter is a poor reader and has trouble with word problems as a result. Should I read them out loud to her?"

It would be wise to discuss this issue with your daughter's teacher. If the teacher approves, you can read the problems to your daughter so she won't miss out on math concepts because of her reading difficulties. The teacher may be willing to make special arrangements for her during tests involving word problems.

❓ "My son is a sixth grader who usually has no trouble with math. But he's having problems understanding and using the metric system. I don't understand it very well myself. How can I help?"

If you aren't familiar with the metric system, take this opportunity to learn it with your child. The relationships within the metric system are easy to follow because they are based on the decimal system.

The units of length, weight, and capacity are the *meter, gram,* and *liter,* respectively. The prefixes *deci-, centi-,* and *milli-* refer to $\frac{1}{10}$, $\frac{1}{100}$, and $\frac{1}{1,000}$ of a unit. The prefixes *deca-, hecto-,* and *kilo-* refer to 10, 100, and 1,000 units.

Your son may be having trouble making mental images of metric measurements. Most people, when they think about a gallon, picture a gallon of milk. Help your son come up with similar images for the metric system. *Examples:*

- A centimeter may be about the size of his thumbnail.

- A liter is a little more than a quart, or half the size of a large-size bottle of soda.

- A gram is about the weight of a large paper clip.

Comparative images like these will be most effective if your son is the one who comes up with them.

How to help your child with math facts and computation

A child who knows math facts can instantly answer addition, subtraction, multiplication, and division number sentences in which two of the numbers are generally one-digit numbers. (*Examples*: 3 + 6, 7 – 2, 8 × 8, 49 ÷ 9.) Before you start teaching math facts to your child, check with the teacher to find out the sequence of lessons for the year. Look through your child's math book when he brings it home, and preview the pages to be learned or worked on before beginning each homework session. Don't encourage your child to work ahead in the book without getting *prior* approval from the teacher.

- As a general rule, teach math facts using low numbers first. There are exceptions; for example, the multiplication tables that are easiest to teach (and learn) are the 0's, 1's, 2's, 5's, 10's, and 11's.

- Use "skip counting"—for example, counting by 2's or 3's—when helping a child learn multiplication.

- Teach related math facts together. For example, "3 + 5" should be taught with "5 + 3," and "8 – 3" should be taught with "8 – 5." Practice gained by filling in addition and multiplication tables can help children discover some of these relationships. See pages 166 and 167 for grids you can copy and use.

- Teach math facts in small doses. As a rule of thumb, three new facts are sufficient for one session.

- Use different formats when teaching math facts. Your child should be able to recognize the same fact regardless of how it's presented. Mix and match these methods:

  - Present the problem orally. (Ask "What's 3 + 4?)

  - Write the problem vertically:

    $$\begin{array}{r} 3 \\ + 4 \\ \hline 7 \end{array}$$

  - Write the problem horizontally:

    $$3 + 4 = 7$$

  - Alternate between writing on paper and writing on flash cards or on a slate or dry-erase board.

- Experiment with possibilities. *Example:* "How many ways can we make 7? There's 3 + 4, and 21 ÷ 3, and 10 – 3, and 7 × 1, and. . . ."

- Review math facts with your child often. Frequent short sessions (ten minutes or so) are usually more effective than infrequent long sessions.

Start helping your child to *overlearn* math facts as soon as they are introduced in class. Often, parents wait to work on these skills until after their child's teacher says that the child is experiencing difficulty. While it's never too late, it's certainly simpler and more pleasant to exercise preventive teaching.

Even after your child appears to know and understand the math facts appropriate to his grade level, they should still be practiced frequently. Aim to "program" them into your child's brain so thoroughly that he can answer problems without stopping to figure them out.

In helping your child with computation, note the following pointers:

- Familiarize yourself with the procedures your child is being taught in school so you don't inadvertently confuse him by using other procedures. For example, in long division, the teacher may want the children to fill in 0's where you were taught to leave empty spaces, like this:

$$\begin{array}{r} 98 \\ 18\overline{)1764} \\ 1620 \\ \hline 144 \\ 144 \\ \hline 000 \end{array}$$

- Some teachers require children to copy problems before working them (a practice often recommended over just filling in blanks on worksheets). Have your child check to see that problems were copied correctly.

- Don't let your child practice a mathematical operation incorrectly. If he's getting wrong answers, ask him to explain how he arrived at the answers. This should help you determine the underlying cause for the difficulty. Possible causes might include insufficient knowledge of math facts, carelessness, and poor understanding of the computation process.

If poor understanding turns out to be the cause, ask the teacher for suggestions. (Also make sure *you* understand the process being taught at school.) Or have your child leave that page or assignment undone. Write a note to the teacher explaining what you think is the source of the problem. This will be a sign to the teacher that further instruction is necessary.

- Resist the urge to correct your child's computation errors. Instead, encourage your child to proofread and correct his own problems. Doing the reverse operation is a preferred way of proofreading. *Example:*

$$
\begin{array}{r} 42 \\ -\ 19 \\ \hline 23 \end{array}
\quad\longleftrightarrow\quad
\begin{array}{r} 23 \\ +\ 19 \\ \hline 42 \end{array}
$$

WHEN TO WORRY ABOUT CHILDREN WHO COUNT ON THEIR FINGERS

Imagine learning to bake a cake without actually doing it. Consider telling someone how to tie a pair of shoelaces without demonstrating it. These tasks would be difficult, if not impossible! So it's understandable that young children in particular need concrete aids when learning math facts and computation. And if there's one thing they can always count on to be there for them, it's their own ten fingers.

The age at which children outgrow counting on their fingers varies from child to child. If your child is still doing it by the third or fourth grade, talk to the teacher and find out what other aids are available. This is especially important if the teacher penalizes children for counting on their fingers.

Making math fun

There are many fun and interesting ways to practice math facts and computation; see Chapter 10 for suggestions. You may want to purchase one or more of the commercial games that teach or reinforce these skills, such as *Yahtzee* or *Mille Bornes*. Flash cards and computer software are other options to explore.

Whenever possible, these skills should be taught in meaningful, real-life contexts. Supervise your child as she makes a minor purchase at a store and keeps the change (counting it afterward to make sure it's right). Open a savings account for your child at a local bank. Let your child take her weekly allowance out of a pile of coins. You can probably think of dozens more fun ways to bring math into your daily activities with your child.

There are also several "tricks" that can take the drudgery out of math facts and computation. (Plus these can serve as a source of pride for your child, since other children may not know them.) *Example:* You might lead your child to discover that adding 9 is the same as adding 10 and taking away 1, or that subtracting 9 is the same as subtracting 10 and adding 1.

Following are more tricks to try with your child.

FOR TEACHING FRACTION REDUCTIONS AND DIVISION

- Numbers that end in a multiple of 2 are divisible by 2. *Examples:* 4, 38, 576, even 1,395,405,778.

- Numbers whose last two digits are a multiple of 4, or whose last three digits are a multiple of 8, are divisible by 4 and 8, respectively. *Example:* Since 56 is divisible by 4, so is 1,356.

- Numbers whose digits add up to multiples of 3 or 9 are divisible by 3 or 9, respectively. *Example:* The digits in 378 add up to 18. Since 18 is divisible by both 3 and 9, so is 378.

- Numbers that end in 5 or 0 are divisible by 5.

- Numbers that end in 0 are divisible by 10.

FOR TEACHING MULTIPLICATION

The "Nines Trick" works for the nines tables. Model it for your child, who will probably be eager to imitate you.

1. Number your fingers from 1 to 10.

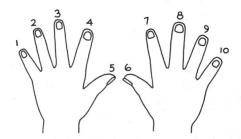

2. Let's say that the problem you want to demonstrate is 9 × 7. Flex the 7 finger. Everything to the *left* of that finger is the tens; everything to the *right* of that finger is the ones. There are 6 fingers to the left and 3 fingers to the right, so the product is 63.

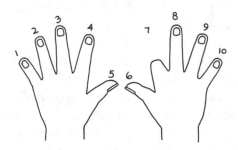

3. This trick can also be used for division when the divisor is 9. For example, to find the answer to 63 ÷ 9, flex the finger that would separate 6 tens from 3 ones. That would be the 7 finger, making the quotient 7.

The "Sluggard's Rule" works when both factors are from 6 to 10 inclusive. (This trick, also called "finger multiplication," was introduced by David van Dantzig in 1941.) It's more difficult than the "Nines Trick" and should be taught only after that trick has been mastered. Your child will need to know the multiplication tables up through 4 × 4 in order to use this trick. Again, you should model it for your child, not just describe it.

1. Start by numbering the fingers on each of your hands from 6 to 10, beginning with the thumbs.

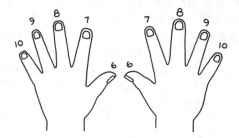

2. To find the product of 8 × 7, touch the 8 finger of one hand to the 7 finger of the other hand. Flex the fingers numbered higher than the two that are touching (the 9 and 10, and the 8, 9, and 10).

3. Add the number of the outstretched fingers (including the two that are touching) to get the tens. Multiply the number of *flexed* fingers on one hand by the number of *flexed* fingers on the other hand to get the ones. In this example, 3 + 2 = 5 for the tens, and 2 × 3 = 6 for the ones, making the product 56.

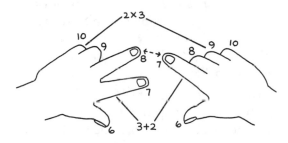

4. For 6 × 6 and 7 × 6, a bit of extra computation is necessary. With 6 × 6 there would be one finger *up* on each hand, making two tens (1 + 1). Then there would be four fingers *flexed* on each hand, making the ones' product 16. This product must be added to the 20 (two tens) for the tens, making the final product 20 + 16 = 36.

This Sluggard's Rule may seem complicated, but never underestimate the child who is desperate to find some "magical" way of figuring out multiplication facts.

▌Resources

Math

Challenge Math Books by Edward Zaccaro (Bellevue, IA: Hickory Grove Press). ***Primary Grade Challenge Math*** (2003) for grades 1 through 4 offers material that goes beyond calculation skills. Includes chapters on problem-solving, money, percents, algebraic thinking, negative numbers, measurements, fractions, division, and much more. ***Challenge Math: For the Elementary and Middle School Student*** (2000) uses fascinating true stories that tie math and science together. Students will be challenged by 1,000 problems at three levels of difficulty. This book allows children to improve their problem-solving skills and see the wondrous side of math and its important role in the world.

Real World Algebra by Edward Zaccaro (Bellevue, IA: Hickory Grove Press, 2001). Just as English can be translated into other languages, word problems can be "translated" into the math language of algebra and easily solved. This book explains this process in an easy-to-understand format using cartoons and drawings. This makes self-learning easy for both the student and any teacher who never did quite understand algebra.

Help!

? **"My daughter is a fifth grader who doesn't know her multiplication facts. She takes forever to do her homework. Should I let her use a calculator?"**

First, find out if her teacher has a plan for helping students master multiplication facts. If so, you can reinforce it at home. If the teacher isn't using a particular plan, have your daughter practice with flash cards. Meanwhile, you can let her use a calculator for long multiplication problems. This will enable her to concentrate on the process without being held back by her lack of knowledge. Once she understands the process, she can return to multiplying on her own and use the calculator to check her answers.

Most children would prefer to do *all* of their math homework on a calculator—not because they're lazy (although this may sometimes be the case), but because calculators are fun to use. Some children will spend blissful hours punching in numbers and watching them appear on the display. To reinforce learning during play, you may want to provide a calculator that functions like an adding machine, printing out whole problems as well as the answers.

"My son needs a lot of help with his math homework, but the terms used in his text are different from the ones I learned in school. I'm discovering, for example, that 'trading,' 'borrowing,' and 'regrouping' can all mean the same thing. How can I help him without confusing him?"

If your son can't define the terms himself, you may be able to check their meanings by looking at the sample problems in his math book or checking the glossary. For your reference, here are some of the most basic terms:

$$\begin{array}{r} \text{addend} \\ +\ \text{addend} \\ \hline \text{sum} \end{array} \qquad \begin{array}{r} \text{factor} \\ \times\ \text{factor} \\ \hline \text{product} \end{array}$$

$$\begin{array}{r} \text{minuend} \\ -\ \text{subtrahend} \\ \hline \text{difference} \end{array}$$

$$\text{divisor}\,\overline{)\,\text{dividend}}^{\ \text{quotient (+ remainder)}}$$

"My son's math homework is sloppy. Since he doesn't line up his numbers correctly, he makes mistakes with two-digit addition and subtraction problems."

Have your son's vision checked by an ophthalmologist or optometrist; his problem may be visual. Or he may be working too fast and just needs to slow down. If his problem is severe, let him use graph paper with large squares, or turn his regular writing paper around so the lines are vertical rather than horizontal. Then have him write numbers between the lines, as in the example shown below. After completing his homework, he can copy the problems on clean paper in the standard fashion.

	3	4
+	4	6
	8	0

"My daughter does well in math, but she sometimes makes careless errors. What can I do?"

CHAPTER 6: MATH **87**

Your daughter should get in the habit of proofreading her work. Review her work and tell her which problems are incorrect. Getting corrective feedback (framed in a positive and encouraging way) is an important part of developing proficiency in mathematics. If she can't spot errors when going over the problems, she can redo the problems on a separate sheet of paper.

Or she can perform the opposite operation and compare her results. For example, a division problem can be proved by multiplying the quotient times the divisor and adding any remainder to obtain the dividend. If the problem is to divide 47 by 7 and she comes up with this answer:

$$\begin{array}{r} 6, \text{ remainder of } 5 \\ 7\overline{)\,47} \\ 42 \\ \hline 5 \end{array}$$

she can check it with this computation:

$$(6 \times 7) + 5 = 47$$

Both redoing problems and performing opposite operations are repetitive and time-consuming tasks. Either may teach your daughter to be more careful the first time around.

"I wanted to know the name of every stone and flower and insect and bird and beast. I wanted to know where it got its color, where it got its life— but there was no one to tell me."

GEORGE WASHINGTON CARVER

7

How to Help Your Child with
Science, Social Studies, and Foreign Languages

What's new in science and social studies instruction?

Science and social studies classes teach children about the world around them and the different people who inhabit this world. Individual schools vary widely in their approach to these two subjects, but both are now guided by national standards.

The National Science Education Standards were developed in 1996 by the National Research Council (*www.nas.edu/nrc*). These standards cover grades K–12 and represent learning in the following areas:

(a) science as inquiry

(b) life sciences

(c) physical sciences

(d) earth and space sciences

(e) science and technology

(f) science in personal and social perspectives

(g) history and nature of science

As you can see, the scope of science education in schools today is quite broad. Teachers now emphasize inquiry, developing an appreciation for the role of science in our lives, and using technology to facilitate the learning of science.

Another piece of "what's new" in science education comes from the No Child Left Behind Act. The act requires states to implement standardized tests in science by the 2007–2008 school year. Check with your school about the schedule for implementation of science standardized testing in your area and ask for tips on helping your child prepare. The National Science Teachers Association Web site provides some excellent tips for parents who want to help their children with science (*www.nsta.org/parents*).

A generation ago, social studies usually meant lessons in history and geography. Today, the subject also includes anthropology, economics, law, political science, philosophy, and sociology. There is a greater emphasis on values and learning about how to make decisions in a diverse, democratic society—and in a shrinking world. To help educators cover this vast subject, standards for social studies were developed by the National Council for the Social Studies (*www.ncss.org*) in 1994. The standards are framed around ten themes:

(1) culture

(2) time, continuity, and change

(3) people, places, and environments

(4) individual development and identity

(5) individuals, groups, and institutions

(6) power, authority, and governance

(7) production, distribution, and consumption

(8) science, technology, and society

(9) global connections

(10) civic ideals and practices

Social studies and science instruction is also moving beyond what you may remember as grades based on the "right" answer. Teachers now focus not only on a right answer (the product) but also on the process—how you arrived at that answer. Thus, you may see your child spend more science time involved in experiments that help him to understand the scientific process—the "hows" and "what ifs."

You may also be called upon to take a more active role in your child's science and social studies education. The importance of parental involvement in these subjects is increasing. You can serve as a model for your child in many ways. When you show curiosity about the world and its people; when you read informational books to your child; when you take your child to the zoo, park, or museum; when you encourage your child to view videos, DVDs, and TV shows related to science and social studies content with you, you are helping your child develop concepts and vocabulary. You are helping your child see the importance of science and social studies in everyday life.

Finally, the resources available for learning about the world are different and improved. Of course, the Internet brings a vast amount of information, but there are also better books on the market than ever.

▌Resources

Science and Social Studies

Don't Know Much About Series—Harper-Collins Publishing *(www.harpercollins.com)*. This growing collection of books by Kenneth C. Davis helps take the boredom out of history, geography, presidents, the solar system, and more.

The Eyewitness Series—DK Publishing *(us.dk.com)*. This book series provides highly visual, descriptive, and engaging books about a wide array of topics: astronomy, archaeology, electricity, ecology, presidents, space, and so on.

NorthWord Books for Young Readers *(www.tnkidsbooks.com/northword.htm)*. These books include picture books and nonfiction nature and wildlife books in interactive and fun-to-read formats. They can be taken to the woods, beach, park, and backyard to help young children learn about the wonders of nature.

HOW THESE CHANGES ARE REFLECTED IN HOMEWORK

Taken together, these changes are likely to mean:

- a balance between homework from textbooks and hands-on learning (that is, more experiments and projects)
- *less* memorization of facts, *more* focus on understanding concepts
- *less* emphasis on the idiosyncrasies of various cultures, *more* emphasis on the interdependence of world cultures

Beyond the three Rs

Learning how to learn about science and social studies requires completely different strategies from what's needed for reading, writing, and arithmetic—the three basic Rs of education. Yet success in science and social studies depends on how well your child has mastered those skills.

Some children who breeze through the three Rs have difficulty with science and social studies. This may be due to a lack of interest, or it may relate to the way science and social studies texts are written and organized. It isn't uncommon for children to perform differently in each subject area. In other words, if your child is brilliant in math, don't assume that she will be equally brilliant in science. (That's equivalent to telling someone, "You can type, so you should be able to play the piano.")

How to help your child with read-the-chapter, answer-the-questions assignments

As early as third grade, children may be required to read chapters in science or social studies books and answer follow-up questions. For children who are accustomed to reading primarily fiction—whether children's literature or the stories in their basal readers—this may prove to be a tedious task.

Reading informational material takes a whole new approach. Among other differences, it requires reading for facts as well as theme and reading more slowly so as not to miss anything important. Informational material tends to be written more densely and may be written at a higher reading level than fiction intended for the same grade. And, frankly, it's often not written very well. It may be grammatically accurate but not very "considerate" of the reader.

The purpose of read-the-chapter, answer-the-questions exercises is to train children to study a body of information for testing at a later date. The following four-step strategy is designed to help your child become comfortable with this process. Start by reading it aloud to your child (including the "Caution" at the end) and modeling it until he gains confidence and proficiency. (For a slightly different approach, look back at pages 55–57.)

1. *Preview the chapter.* Skim through it quickly before actually starting to read it. Previewing means:

- reading the chapter headings and subheadings

- reading the introduction

- reading the summary at the end

- looking at graphs, tables, charts, maps, and other illustrations

- checking out features like the index and the glossary, which may guide you to some of the answers you need to find

Previewing helps you budget your reading time by giving you an idea of how long the chapter is and whether you're familiar with the subject matter. If the chapter is long, you may want to read it in more than one sitting. If it contains many new and difficult words, chunk it into small pieces and tackle them one at a time.

(PARENTS: This step may require some advance preparation. For example, your child may ignore the legend at the bottom of a chart or a map and misunderstand it entirely. Or your child may not understand the purpose of the index or glossary. You may want to begin by paging through the book, pointing out the various parts, and explaining them in simple language.)

2. *Read the questions.* Read them all the way through, looking up any words you don't know.

3. *Read the chapter carefully.*

4. *Answer the questions, looking back through the chapter whenever you need to.* If you're supposed to write the answers in complete sentences, be sure to check your capitalization and punctuation.

C A U T I O N

DON'T, repeat, DON'T get in the habit of using the "search-and-destroy" approach to these assignments. In other words, DON'T read the questions first and then skim the chapter to find the answers. If you don't give the chapter a THOROUGH reading, you may miss important facts and concepts you need for tests.

Help!

? **"Science and social studies have never been my strong suit. I steered clear from science in school and still don't consider myself strong in geography or history. How can I possibly help my daughter with these subjects?"**

You don't have to be a scientist or geography whiz to help your daughter with these subjects. Having an open mind and exploring these topics with her is all that is required.

Following are some myths and countering facts that the National Science Teachers Association *(www.nsta.org/explore4)* has identified about science education. The facts hold true for social studies education as well.

- "Myth #1: Science is difficult"—Fact: Science and social studies are just really learning about the world in which we live.

- "Myth #2: You need to know a lot about science to teach it to your children"—Fact: Learning about science and social studies is an opportunity to learn together.

- "Myth #3: Science requires equipment"—Fact: Science and social studies are all around us; no intensive equipment is required.

- "Myth #4: Science skills should wait for reading skills"—Fact: Start building curiosity about our world and the people who live in it early and often.

? **"My daughter isn't in the highest reading group in her class, but she** still has to use the same science book those students use. There is no way that she can complete her assignments by herself; her reading skills aren't up to it. Should I help her by reading the chapters out loud to her?"**

If the text is really too difficult for her, talk to the teacher. If the teacher insists that your daughter participate with the rest of the class in using this text, you may need to read the chapters to her.

? **"My son always gets A's on his daily work in history, but he rarely passes the tests. How can he answer questions correctly on his daily work but not remember the answers when test time comes?"**

He may be using the "search-and-destroy" method to answer the questions in his daily work. Encourage your son to read the chapter carefully before trying to answer the questions. A quick review the night or morning before the test will help, too.

? **"My son never reads his geography chapter before starting to answer the questions at the end. Yet he seems to get all the answers right, and he also does well on tests. Should I still insist that he read the chapters carefully?"**

Perhaps the teacher lectures right from the text or allows class time for reading the chapters. Ask and find out. On the other hand, your son may already know the material being covered. As long as he's doing such a good job, let him continue in the same manner. (Remember the old saying "If it isn't broken, don't fix it!") Keep an eye on him in the future, though, when other teachers' styles may require him to do more work on his own.

How to help your child study chapters for tests

Knowing how to study chapters for tests is vital, since your child will be required to do this through high school and beyond. Relatively few children can read a chapter once and retain all the information needed for a test; most need to practice more intense study methods. Look back at pages 25–27 for suggestions on helping your child. Following are more techniques to try.

If studying for a test has been preceded by a "read-the-chapter, answer-the-questions" exercise, half of the work has been done already. If not, the study session should begin with a preview and careful reading of the chapter, as described on pages 91–93. Even if your child has carefully read the whole chapter once, a methodical rereading may be necessary to prepare for a test. Here is a good procedure to follow:

1. Have your child read each paragraph or section, then stop.

2. Now have your child try to project one or two questions the teacher might ask about the paragraph or section.

3. Record these questions on individual index cards (flash cards), with the answers on the back.

4. After your child has finished rereading the entire chapter, make additional flash cards for any follow-up questions that cannot be answered immediately.

5. Finally, make flash cards for new vocabulary words introduced in the chapter.

Once these first five steps have been accomplished, the *real* studying can begin:

6. Go over the flash cards until your child can give the answers automatically. Given enough drill-and-practice, her memory should "kick in" even if test anxiety sets in.

7. If you know what format the test will take—matching, fill-in-the-blanks, short answer, and so on—try to construct a sample test with your child. (This can be especially beneficial for children who have high test anxiety.)

This process takes time and commitment on your part and your child's. But it works—and often results in improved grades.

MAKING STUDYING FUN

Studying for tests will *not* be fun if you and your child start too late. From the very first day of the new school year, emphasize to your child that she *must* let you know about a test as soon as it is announced in class. (You may want to use one of the Assignment Sheets on pages 144 or 145 to record test dates and relevant information.) Once you hear about a test, you and your child can plan your study time accordingly. Many games can be adapted to studying for chapter tests. See Chapter 10 for suggestions.

Help!

"There is absolutely no way that my son can make up sample test questions! He has a hard enough time just reading the chapter, much less understanding it well enough to invent questions."

Your son needs you to model this for him. Start by reading the chapter with him, paragraph by paragraph. Then have your son make up a question while you make one up at the same time. Record the questions on flash cards. Don't expect miracles overnight, but your son should gradually become familiar enough with the kinds of questions his teacher asks that he can begin constructing his own.

❓ "My daughter can understand chapter material fairly easily, but her attention span is very short. The night before a test, she is in misery studying the chapters. The chapters are just too long."

Your daughter needs to study well in advance of a test—not only the night before. As soon as a chapter is assigned, have her chunk it into smaller portions, then read and study one portion each night. This eliminates the last-minute cramming routine that most children find frustrating and scary.

❓ "My daughter never needs to study for tests. The most she ever has to do is quickly read over a chapter the night before. I'm afraid that when she encounters more difficult material in higher grades or college, she will fall apart. Shouldn't she form the habit *now* of studying more carefully?"

Your daughter's manner of studying may carry her through high school, college, and beyond. However, it isn't uncommon for outstanding elementary and middle school students to run into trouble later, when they are asked to master more difficult materials. If your daughter is serious about her grades, you may want to enroll her in a study skills course so she will be ready to adjust her study habits if and when this becomes necessary.

How to help your child with graphics

Much of the material in science and social studies texts is presented in the form of maps, charts, timelines, and graphs. Formal instruction in graphics other than maps typically begins in the third grade and continues through junior high school; it may be included as part of the math, reading, science, and/or social studies curriculum. Even so, some children continue to have difficulty interpreting graphics or fail to see their importance. This is especially true if reading is a chore for them. They concentrate so hard on the text that they don't have any energy left over for the graphics.

Map-reading skills may be introduced as early as kindergarten. Instruction usually begins with the concepts of near/far, up/down, and above/below and gradually moves to complex concepts like the international date line, map scale, and map projection/distortion. (These are normally covered by the sixth grade.) Often, map concepts take root slowly and are hard for children to grasp. Many third-grade students, for example, are amazed to learn that we do not live "inside" the earth. Others regularly confuse cities with states and continents with countries.

One good way to help your child understand graphic materials is through the use of graphs on a computer. Another way is to encourage and assist him in making maps, graphs, timelines, and so on with construction paper, crayons, colorful markers, rulers, and other interesting tools. Hands-on experience is not only fun; it also enables children to comprehend the reasons for graphics and the ways they are produced.

MAPS

Here are some ways you can help your child improve his map skills:

- Find out the sequence of map skills taught in your child's class. If your child is experiencing difficulty, perhaps he hasn't yet mastered the prerequisite skills. Ask the teacher for suggestions you can use at home.

- Many children have trouble with the concept of distance. For example, one ten-year-old boy I tutored couldn't comprehend the idea of driving one hundred miles in a car because he had never been for a ground "trip" that was longer than a five-mile ride from his home to the airport. You can instill a sensitivity to distance with activities like these:

  - Walk a mile with your child; then show him how a mile is represented on a map.

  - Ask your child to keep track of the odometer reading during car trips. (If you have a "trip meter," set it to zero at the beginning for an exact count of the miles traveled.) Then show him how that distance is represented on a road map.

  - Orient your child to the four cardinal directions. Go outside and point out North, South, East, and West. If you have a compass, use it to demonstrate direction. (You may want to buy your child a compass of his own; kids love gadgets like these.) Be patient when helping your child learn these concepts.

- Relative location—the location of one place in relation to another—can also be difficult for children to grasp. Using a map with a compass, ask your child a series of questions like these:

  - "What direction is _____ from _____?"

  - "Is _____ north or south of _____?"

  - "If you were going from _____ to _____, in what direction would you be traveling?"

- Encourage your child to read a map legend carefully before attempting to answer any questions about the map.

- Determine the meaning of any other symbols on the map and help your child discover how and where they are used.

- Refresh your own knowledge of map-related vocabulary. Your child may be asked to locate a continent, a peninsula, or a strait on a map without having any inkling of what those terms mean.

- Keep an atlas and a globe at home (perhaps in your child's study center) and use them frequently—to add meaning to coin and stamp collections, when reading stories about other lands, and so on. If your child has access to the Internet or a CD-ROM with geographical information, so much the better!

C A U T I O N

If your child is colorblind, he may have special difficulty with color-coded maps. Be sure that the teacher is aware of this condition early in the school year.

GRAPHS, DIAGRAMS, AND TABLES

Graphs, diagrams, and tables are common graphics. Here are some helpful tips when teaching your child to use these aids:

- Identify the title of the graphic and discuss what information is being illustrated.

- When working with a graph, start by identifying what kind it is: pie graph, line graph, bar graph, or pictograph. Examples of each are shown on page 98.

- Read line graphs, bar graphs, pictographs, tables, and charts from the "outside in." In other words, look first at any headings at the top, the bottom, and along both sides before moving to the information contained in the graphic.

- When working with a graph or a timeline, identify the unit of measure used. *Examples:* inch, foot, or mile; day, week, month, or year; quantity.

- When working with a diagram, determine how it is labeled. *Example:* A skeleton may have labels for each bone.

- Determine the meanings of any symbols on the graphic.

- Discuss ways in which the graphic can be used. *Examples:* A graphic of toy sales before and after the holidays can help store owners decide how many toys to stock each month and how many cash registers to keep open. An airplane schedule is a table used by airport employees, passengers, and persons taking passengers to or from the airport.

- Take turns with your child inventing questions that can be answered by studying the graphic.

MAKING GRAPHICS FUN

- Play games that stress geography and graphic skills mastery. See Chapter 10 for suggestions.

- Develop "graphics radar." Both you and your child can keep an eye out for graphics in your everyday routines, and then discuss them together. The national newspaper *USA Today* is an excellent resource for clear, colorful maps, charts, and graphs of all kinds.

- If your child is a sports fan, keep a map handy so he can locate the home cities of favorite teams. When watching sports events, use a map or globe to locate the countries, cities, and continents mentioned during the competition.

- If your child is an animal fancier, locate the countries and continents that are the original homes of his favorite animals. On trips to the zoo, take a small world map along for the same purpose.

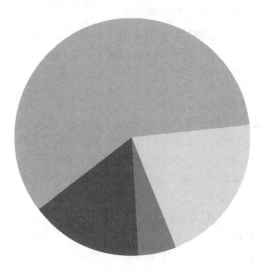

Pie Graph

Line Graph

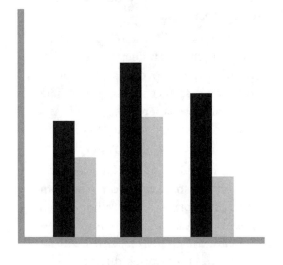

Bar Graph

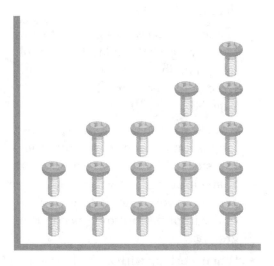

Pictograph

- When planning a family trip, help your child locate your destination on a map. If you'll be traveling by plane, discuss how long it would take to get there by car. When touring a city, locate points of interest on a city map (available from most boards of tourism or information offices or kiosks).

- Send away for a map of your child's favorite amusement or theme park. Learning map-reading skills is fun when the map is colorful and exciting.

- Purchase a large, colorful floor or wall map of the world and place it in your child's room or study center.

- Most shopping malls provide centrally located maps of their stores and shops. The next time you go shopping with your child, lead him to one of these maps. Then let your child lead *you* from one store to another.

- Many children enjoy keeping behavior charts on a daily basis. Let your child construct his own chart for tracking chores done, homework completed, numbers of books read, math facts mastered, and so on. Record progress with check marks or stickers.

- Make a "pedigree chart" showing the lineage of your family, or make a family timeline. (These can also be nice gifts for relatives.)

Help!

"My son is in the fifth grade. His next science test is going to be on the human skeletal system. His teacher will give him a diagram of the skeleton, and he'll have to label the bones. How can I help him prepare?"

Make multiple photocopies of a *clear* picture or drawing of a skeleton and have your son practice writing in the correct name for each bone. It may take many repetitions before he knows them all (which is why you'll need multiple photocopies), so be patient and encouraging. If you can come up with any mnemonics, or "memory tricks" (for example, "Elvis the pelvis"), so much the better.

"My daughter got a D on her last social studies test. She told me that she had read the chapter carefully and didn't understand why her grade was so low. We looked over the questions she missed and discovered that the information she needed to know was in the chapter, but it was presented in charts and timelines rather than the text. My daughter claims that she 'skipped those parts' because she didn't think they were important."

This isn't at all uncommon. Many children perceive graphics as "free spaces" in reading and just advance to the next paragraph. Communicate to your daughter the importance of graphic information, using the suggestions given on pages 95–99.

"My son never has trouble reading graphs, diagrams, or maps of any kind. How can I encourage him to develop this talent further?"

Why not name him the "Official Navigator" on family vacations? This will give him the opportunity to put his skills to work in real-life situations. Allow him plenty of time in advance to study the maps you'll be using; if he's responsible for reading them under pressure or during times of peak traffic, or if he makes an error and you take a wrong turn, you'll both get frustrated.

You can also encourage your son to include graphics in his school reports and projects. Creating graphics may be time-consuming (especially without the aid of computer graphics software), but they add that "something extra" that children enjoy—and teachers often reward.

? **"My daughter doesn't like science and thinks it's really for boys. What can I do to encourage her to get interested in science?"**

Expose her to the world of female scientists. You can start by leading her to biographies of women who have made their mark in science. Following is a starter list to use as you search the library or the Internet for information:

- Anthropologist Margaret Mead
- Anthropologist Mary Douglas Leakey
- Astronaut Eileen Collins
- Astronaut Ellen Ochoa
- Astronaut Judith Resnik
- Astronaut Sally Ride
- Astronomer Margaret Burbidge
- Astronomer Carolyn Shoemaker
- Aviator and sailor Marion Rice Hart
- Biologist Rachel Carson
- Chemist Rachel Fuller Brown
- Chemist Marie Curie
- Chemist Dorothy Crowfoot Hodgkin
- Civil engineer Elsie Eaves

- Computer scientist Grace Brewster Murray Hopper
- Conservationist Joy Gessner Adamson
- Cosmonaut Valentina Tereshkova
- Geneticist Barbara McClintock
- Geologist Doris Malkin Curtis
- Microbiologist Alice Evans
- Nobel Prize–winner Gertrude Elion
- Nuclear physicist Rosalyn Yalow
- Physician (and former U.S. Surgeon General) Joycelyn Elders
- Physician Myra Adele Logan
- Physician (and former U.S. Surgeon General) Antonia Novello
- Physicist Mary Beth Stearns
- Primatologist Dian Fossey
- Primatologist Jane Goodall
- Psychiatrist Elisabeth Kübler-Ross

Also, check out these Web sites: 4,000 Years of Women in Science (*www.astr.ua. edu/4000ws*) and Historia (*www.women-scientists-in-history.com*).

How to help your child with thematic units

Thematic units are a multidisciplinary route to learning. If you look at the themes for standards in science and social studies, you can see that there's an emphasis on linking content areas. Teachers who use thematic units spend a great deal of time planning their academic subjects around a theme such as space, insects, or electricity.

Although this planning is quite a challenge, teachers need to make certain that all district-level curriculum objectives are included during the year. Many teachers who use thematic units believe that the time and effort are worth it. Students benefit because their learning is connected, meaningful, memorable, and exciting. Some thematic units—such as those on gun safety or cultural heritage—are taught school wide or district wide.

Writing expert Lucy Calkins and her colleagues like to tell parents, "Your child's reading, writing, and theme studies will spill over into your home this year . . . and we want their obsessions and passions and projects to spill over from the home into the classroom as well." They hope and expect that children will consciously and deliberately weave literacy together with the passions, projects, and people of their lives. A good way to help this happen is by getting involved with theme studies in your child's classroom. You might provide resources for the teacher to use, or you might find ways to extend one or more themes into your family activities. Ask the teacher for a list of themes your child's class will be exploring, along with a schedule of when they will be featured during the year. Then tailor the suggestions on pages 101–103 to fit the thematic unit your child is currently experiencing.

Help!

? **"The science and social studies programs at my daughter's school are confusing to me. I hear about weekly lessons on tree planting and drug awareness, but I'm concerned that I hear nothing about geography or history or earth science."**

Most districts will have a comprehensive scope-and-sequence plan for science and social studies into which these units can be integrated. Ask about the curriculum at your school and how your child's teacher is planning to cover the instructional objectives.

? **"I'm thinking of boycotting the science fair this year. It seems like it is all parent work."**

Science fair projects can be fun and a fabulous learning experience for children. Yet they can also be a nightmare. Parent involvement in science fairs is sometimes encouraged, sometimes not. Check with your child's teacher about his or her philosophy. If the teacher wants parental involvement, look at the exercise as an opportunity to teach your child how to plan and take responsibility for a long-term project. Suggestions for doing this are provided in Chapter 8.

12 ways to build your child's fund of general information

Children who have a rich fund of general information and background knowledge on a variety of subjects will find science and social studies (and reading and writing) easier and more interesting than those who don't. As a caring parent, you have the privilege and the responsibility of sharing the world with your child.

Describe your own childhood experiences, the things that interested you then (and interest you now), your favorite places, and whatever else occurs to you. Be ready at a moment's notice to answer your child's questions—or promise to help her find the answers if you don't know them yourself. Talk, talk, talk—about feelings, hobbies, politics, advertisements, TV shows, music, roller skates, road signs, poems, movies, grandparents, pets, anything and everything! And listen, listen, listen to your child.

A child who's treated as someone worth talking to develops a sense of value and self-respect. A child who's treated as someone worth listening to develops strong verbal skills and an undying curiosity. And both of you together develop better communication and a deeper understanding of each other's wants and needs, hopes and dreams, personalities and beings. The more you converse with each other, the more rewarding your conversations and your relationship will become.

Here are suggestions for stimulating activities to enjoy with your child. Talk about them before; talk about them during; talk about them after!

1. Check public radio and television listings for news, documentaries, and other interesting programs; then listen and watch together.

2. Read informational books to and with your child. Many parents stick to storybooks and wait to introduce informational text when children are older. Don't wait. Informational books abound for preschoolers and beyond.

3. If you have access to the Internet, explore various Web sites with your child, such as

those listed on pages 123–124. You may also want to use the following sites: "The Parents' Guide to the Information Superhighway (*www.childrenspartnership.org*) or "Parent's Guide to the Internet (*www.ed.gov/pubs/parents/internet*). See also Chapter 9 for additional Internet resources.

4. When renting or buying videos or DVDs for home viewing, include educational topics.

5. Take your child to natural history museums, science museums, art museums, children's museums, zoos, botanical gardens, historical sites, and more.

6. Take your child to national parks and forests and go on tours with the rangers.

7. Have your child read articles in a newspaper or in news magazines, or read them aloud to her.

8. Take *frequent* trips to the public library. (Jim Trelease, the author of *The Read-Aloud Handbook*, asks parents to think about their priorities by comparing the number of times they take their kids to the library versus the number of times they take them to the shopping mall.) If your child is mature enough and has developed library skills, you can go to the library together and arrange to meet in a certain place at a certain time (an hour later, for example). Then let her have the run of the place. One child I know was eagerly scanning microfiche when he was still too short to reach it without standing on a chair. And he knew from an early age how to ask librarians for directions and suggestions. His idea of a "fun night out" was an evening spent at the library!

9. Make vacations learning experiences. Read travel guides together and let your child participate in the where-to-go, what-to-see decision-making process.

10. Watch *quality* movies with your child; then discuss them afterward. Don't limit your choices to commercial theaters. Check out movies offered at libraries, museums, and other cultural centers. And don't restrict your choices to current movies. If you have a VCR or DVD player, use it to screen old comedies, historical dramas, and adventures.

11. Plan "theme" birthday parties with your child that involve some research. *Examples:* an American Revolution costume party; an Inventor's Convention; a play.

12. Take advantage of every "teachable moment" that presents itself during a normal day: trips to the grocery store, gardening, walks around the block, meal preparation, dinnertime discussions, and many, many more.

Remember: Your child is eager to learn. *And you are your child's most important teacher.*

Help!

"There are books in our local bookstore about everything my child should know in each grade. Should I buy these books and drill my child on this material?"

Research has shown that information learned in small, isolated bits is quickly forgotten. Rather than investing your time (and money) on books like these, expose your child to an ever-increasing fund of information, as described on pages 101–103.

"When should I start exposing my son to informational books? We have lots of storybooks at home. Should I wait until my son is more mature to introduce books about science, social studies, etc.?"

We are learning more and more about the importance of introducing children to informational text at an early age. Even before your son learns to read, picture books and concept books are good starting points for informational text. Exposing your child to informational text will not only help him learn concepts and vocabulary; it will also familiarize him with expository text—the primary language of school textbooks.

How to help your child with foreign languages

In elementary school, foreign languages have traditionally been taught for enrichment. As countries become more multicultural and the world becomes more interdependent, the need to speak more than one language is increasing. In most elementary schools, the foreign language teacher is a specialist who visits the elementary classroom once, twice, or more often during the week. The curriculum varies greatly. If your child is given the opportunity to receive foreign language instruction, start by finding out about the program. Ask questions like these:

- "How often will the class meet?"
- "How intensive will the instruction be?"

- "What kinds of things will my child be learning?"

- "Will homework be required? If so, what can I do to help at home?"

Like one's native language, a foreign language is learned more by practice and "absorption" than by any conscious effort to master the rules of grammar. (In any event, these come later, not in the elementary curriculum.) Television, videos and DVDs, audiocassettes, CDs, foreign language clubs, and pen pals can aid your child's practice. Naturally, the preferred way to learn a language is to live in a country where it is spoken, but this is not an option for most young children. If you're planning a foreign vacation anyway, you may want to consider visiting a country where your child can hear the language he is studying. You might also explore exchange student programs. If your school doesn't keep a file of exchange program addresses, contact the embassy of a country whose people speak the language you're interested in.

An important point to remember when helping your child with a foreign language is *not to overcorrect*. Children who are learning English are allowed to experiment—for example, with "ed" as the past tense form of all verbs, including "runned." Children who are learning a foreign language should be given the same leeway.

MAKING LANGUAGE LEARNING FUN

Learning about other cultures can be fascinating. Here are several suggestions to try with your child:

- Read to your child about life in the country (or countries) where people speak the language he's learning.

- If you have friends from that country (or countries), ask them to spend some time talking with your child.

- Seek out articles in *National Geographic* and travel magazines (the more pictures, the better).

- Volunteer to assist with international fairs at your child's school.

- Obtain posters and other small items from travel agents or import shops.

- Visit a local restaurant that specializes in foods of the country.

- Talk to friends around the world on the Internet.

- Try using games, especially if you can speak the language. Work with your child to make flash cards of the words he is learning. Since most of these will have to do with animals, foods, colors, people, and actions, make word-and-picture cards for playing Concentration (see pages 133–134) or Wet Cat (a game similar to Old Maid). Make cards to teach vocabulary from the language and facts about the countries where it is spoken; then use a trivia board game to track progress and keep score.

- Use your imagination!

Help!

? **"My daughter is a good student and is taking Spanish in school. However, she isn't at all motivated to practice the phrases she's assigned for homework."**

Talk with the teacher to determine the reason for your daughter's "couldn't care less" attitude. She may be afraid to take risks, which studying a foreign language certainly demands. She may be hesitant to pronounce the new words for fear of being ridiculed. Or she may be finding that foreign languages don't come as easily to her as other subjects.

Start by relaxing any demands you are currently making on her to "do well" in Spanish class. Instead, emphasize the value and fun of learning a new language. Make an effort to learn the words she is being taught so the two of you can have mini-conversations. She may feel more encouraged to take risks if you demonstrate that you are.

If these approaches are unsuccessful, it may be wise to let your daughter discontinue her Spanish instruction until she is older and perhaps more interested. Although some aspects of language learning are easier when one is very young, this is not true for all aspects. Plus learning is easier when motivation is higher. Instead of spoiling any desire your daughter might have to learn a foreign language in the future, let it go for now.

"My son has difficulty reading in English, and now he's also being taught to read in French. Will this cause a problem?"

Knowledge of two languages generally promotes conceptual development in both, and this development is directly related to reading skills. So studying French shouldn't hurt your son. However, if he continues to have a hard time reading English, he should take a second language only if the emphasis is on speaking rather than reading.

"My son is excited about learning French and is picking up oral French easily. But he has problems reading in French, and this problem prevents him from completing his homework."

Your son is mastering the most difficult aspect of the new language, for which he should be praised and encouraged. You might want to find out whether his teacher or an advanced student could record his homework on audiocassette so he can read and listen simultaneously. Some of the suggestions for improving reading skills found in Chapters 3 and 4 might also be helpful here.

"My daughter does well on her weekly Spanish quizzes, but she has difficulty with tests that cover several units. It seems that while she's learning the material in one unit, she's forgetting everything she learned before."

Your daughter needs to review previous lessons on a regular basis. Learning a foreign language is a cumulative process; you can't just learn the new and "dump" the old. You can help her to review by adapting the suggestions found on pages 94–95.

"My son studies with a friend every evening. They practice their Spanish together, but neither uses a very good Spanish accent. Should I let them continue?"

Be glad that your son is practicing and progressing without your overt assistance. The only help you should offer is to provide videos or DVDs, audiocassettes, or CDs to expand their practice. In time, their accents should improve.

"I make them believe in themselves."

JAIME ESCALANTE

8

How to Help Your Child with

Formal Assessments, Projects, Reports, and Papers

How to help your child prepare for standardized tests

As a result of the No Child Left Behind Act, states are required to test students annually in the areas of mathematics and reading or language arts, and eventually science.

Standardized tests are designed to compare an individual student's score to the scores of other students at the state and national level. There are many purposes for standardized tests, including evaluation of state and local programs, performance of individual schools, and performance of individual students to determine promotion. Following are tips to help you prepare your child for these important tests. The National

Education Association *(www.nea.org/par ents)* and the National PTA *(www.pta.org/ parentinvolvement/helpchild/index.asp)* offer additional tips and suggestions to help your child get ready.

STANDARDIZED TESTS OF READING AND MATH

Preparation for standardized reading and math tests is an ongoing process. Children who read a lot and are read to regularly, who think through problems, and who have good attention spans are more likely to do better on standardized tests than other children. In addition to the continuous preparation inherent in the suggestions throughout this book, you can help your child in the following ways:

- If homework involves multiple-choice answers, have your child explain why one answer is correct *and* why the others are incorrect.

- When your child practices math facts, be sure that she writes them both horizontally and vertically.

- When your child is reading (or you're reading to your child), have her tell you the main idea or what the story or selection is mostly about.

- Expose your child to new vocabulary. Use interesting words when you talk to her, and read aloud from books that introduce new words.

- Take turns with your child asking and answering questions about material that has been read, allowing for "look backs" to find the answers.

You might also use homework that involves multiple-choice answers as test-taking practice. Here's how:

1. Read each possible answer *with* the stem. This helps your child focus on the right answer to the given question. For this question . . .

> Many children like:
>
> A. pizza
>
> B. hamburgers
>
> C. ice cream
>
> D. all of the above.

. . . you would say, "Many children like pizza. Many children like hamburgers. Many children like ice cream. Many children like all of the above."

2. Model reading *all* choices before choosing an answer, explaining out loud why each choice seems to be right or wrong. *Example:* "'Many children like pizza.' That's true, so maybe that's the right answer. But let's try the next ones to make sure they aren't the right answers. 'Many children like hamburgers.' 'Many children like ice cream.' Those are true, too! This may be a tough one! Let's see. The last choice is, 'Many children like all of the above.' Ah, that's the right answer!"

3. Show your child how to use the process of elimination. *Example:* "If B, C, and D are definitely wrong, then the answer must be A."

WRITING TO A PROMPT

Your child may receive formal writing assessment beginning in the intermediate grades. With such assessment, children may be instructed to write to a given prompt. (*Examples:* "Pretend you woke up one morning and found yourself to be two inches tall. Tell about your day." "Explain how to make a peanut butter sandwich.") The "score" for such an assessment—often a number from one to six—will combine all areas of writing, from content to spelling and grammar.

The best way to prepare for this type of assessment is to encourage your child to spend time writing each day. Time spent working on revisions is also valuable. You can help directly by having frequent conversations with your child about writing strengths and possibilities for improvement. See also the suggestions given in Chapter 5. Your child's composition homework provides further practice that will strengthen the skills evaluated in a formal writing assessment. Try the following ideas:

- Ask the teacher if there is a rubric, or scoring system, you can have so you can see what areas of writing are assessed in your child's classroom. (See the sample rubric on page 71.)

- On a regular basis, celebrate fine turns of phrase in material read by you or your child. This provides excellent modeling.

- Use a highlighter to note any exceptional word choices your child makes in her writing (*example:* "lionhearted" instead of "brave").

- Let your child write on a computer, if one is available. If not, have her write on every other line of the paper to allow for easy revision.

- When your child is given a topic to write about, help her stay on topic.

- Review your child's final drafts to be sure they are organized from beginning to end.

- Help ensure that your child adds supporting details for her ideas.

- Once the above areas are addressed, focus on spellings of commonly misspelled words (for example, because, a lot, too, their) and on basic punctuation and grammar.

C A U T I O N

Children's tolerance for revision varies. If your child's tolerance is minimal, go only as far as you can with these suggestions without causing undue discomfort to your child (and to you).

CONQUERING TEST ANXIETY

You might think of test anxiety as a bell-shaped curve. At one end are test-takers who are too anxious and consequently don't do well; at the other are test-takers who couldn't care less about how they perform. A moderate degree of anxiety will produce the best results. To encourage an appropriate amount of test anxiety in your child (and discourage panic or indifference), try these suggestions:

1. Occasionally have your child complete her homework with a timer and without any help so she becomes accustomed to working under test-like conditions.

2. Teach your child to take brief "relaxation breaks" if she starts getting too anxious. *Example:* "Close your eyes. Breathe deeply. Think about tensing, then relaxing every part of your body, from your toes to the top of your head."

3. Consider taking your child out for a special breakfast on the day of an important test. I know of one parent who did this for her child's first standardized test so the child would have positive associations with testing.

How to help your child with special projects

Art fair, science fair, social studies displays! Special projects are a welcome diversion from daily worksheets and textbook assignments—but they can also be a nightmare for parents. If your child doesn't quite know what to do or how to do it, *you* could end up bearing the burden.

There is a way to achieve more child participation and less parental involvement, and it's called *planning*. As soon as the assignment is made, you and your child should sit down to discuss it and plot out a project plan. The following list of steps can get you started. You can copy and use the checklist on pages 168–169.

1. Decide on the project theme.

2. Have the theme approved by the teacher.

3. Make a list of things that need to be done and the order in which they should be completed.

4. Decide who is going to do what.

5. Set deadlines for completing each part of the project.

6. Make a list of the materials needed.

7. Make a projected budget.

8. Send away for resource materials needed.

9. Contact community resources.

10. Conduct research at the library and on the Internet.

11. Complete the project on schedule.

Special projects can be fun, *if* children are allowed to choose themes that interest them and *if* they are encouraged (not smothered) by parental supervision. As you work with your child, lend your support when it is needed and when it is asked for. Avoid the temptation to do the project for your child. (We shouldn't hear parents ask each other, "What did *you* get on the science fair project?") Your child can experience joy in a job well done—and independently done.

If you have Internet access, this can add a new and exciting dimension to special projects. Here you and your child can find a wealth of information on any topic imaginable. Start by exploring the sites listed on pages 123–124. Ask the teacher and your school or district media specialist for more recommendations. (See also the guidelines for using the Internet on pages 122–123.)

Help!

? **"My daughter doesn't have any ideas for her science fair experiment. I have no clue about what's**

appropriate and what isn't. **Where can we go to get ideas?"**

Look around you. You may find inspiration in the kitchen for experiments on heat, refrigeration, or decay. You may find inspiration in the garden for experiments on plant or insect development. For additional ideas, talk to a librarian—or a friendly scientist in your community. Or turn to one of these resources:

Complete Handbook of Science Fair Projects by Julianne Blair Bochinski (New York: Wiley, 2003).

Janice VanCleave's Guide to More of the Best Science Fair Projects by Janice VanCleave (New York: Wiley, 2000).

100 Amazing Make-It-Yourself Science Fair Projects by Glen Vecchione (New York: Sterling Publishing Co., 2005).

"Last year my son was supposed to make a social studies display, but I did all the work. I refuse to do it again this year. What can I do to get him involved?"

Follow the steps on page 110. Decide first what needs to be done, then who is going to do it. Because you're trying to limit your involvement, confine your contributions to tasks like providing transportation to the library, proofreading a first draft, or supplying opportunities for your son to earn money to cover the cost of the project. See page 170 for a form the two of you can use to make your arrangement "official."

"My son can't draw. Last year his social studies poster was a disaster! Should I do it for him this year?"

If your son is truly embarrassed by his inability to draw, perhaps his teacher can suggest another format for the poster. For example, if you have access to a computer graphics program (and it's one your son can learn to use), this may be the solution.

"Last year at our school, the science fair consisted mostly of *parent* projects. My daughter completed her project all by herself, and it was obviously not as polished as the others. Should I help her more this year?"

Independence is the primary goal of any special project. If your daughter is content to complete her project on her own, more power to her. Be available to serve as a resource, but continue to foster her independent spirit. In other words, hands off!

How to help your child with book reports

Schools today are on a reading bandwagon. Teachers are encouraging students to read, read, and read some more. Principals often set reading goals and incentives for the student body. If students read enough books, some principals are even willing to sit on a rooftop or get slimed. Many schools have special events focused on reading such as book fairs, parent reading nights, or even reading pajama parties.

It isn't unusual for elementary school children to be required to complete a book each week or (in upper grades) a longer, more substantial book each month. As a caring parent, you can support this excellent emphasis on reading by taking regular trips to the library or bookstore with your child and by planning regular family reading times. Given the choice, most children will opt to rent the video, DVD, or audiocassette over reading the book. Don't give the choice. Insist that multimedia aids be used as supplements rather than substitutes for the real thing.

In many classrooms today, the formal book report is a thing of the past. Instead, children are required to complete alternate assignments to give evidence of having read a book. Posters, puppets, and plays have supplanted written reports, with some teachers devising a variety of creative options. Many teachers who still assign book reports provide a format for children to follow. If your child is assigned a book report, and if the teacher doesn't provide a format, the outlines on pages 171–182 can serve as frameworks for writing reports on three different kinds of books: fiction, non-fiction, and biography.

A book report is generally perceived as something to slog through. (You probably don't have especially fond memories from your own childhood where book reports are concerned.) They may not be the most fascinating and stimulating of all assignments, but they do serve several purposes. They get children reading, and they get them reading *carefully*. If children know that they're going to have to write about something they read, they're less likely to skim it. A good book report format also trains a child to pay attention to details like setting, characters, and plot.

The most critical factor in making a book report more bearable is finding a proper match between a book and a child.

Help your child select a book that is both interesting and readable. Ask your school or public librarian for suggestions. Find out if the teacher has a list of recommended books that are likely to appeal to your child. If your child is assigned a book and is not given the luxury of choosing, help him plan enough time to complete it. Work reading assignments into his homework schedule or incorporate them into your family reading time.

Help!

"My son is required to hand in a book report every other week. It's a constant hassle at our house. The night before the report is due, we're always pushing him to get it done. Isn't this too severe an assignment for a fifth grader?"

If the book report is always being done the night before it's due, then it is "too severe" an assignment—for you and your family. Help your son select books that are interesting to him and are written at a comfortable level of difficulty. Then help him establish a reading schedule that enables him to complete his reading early. Two nights before the report is due, encourage him to write a rough draft. Work with him to proofread it and find and correct any errors. The night before the report is due, he can complete the final draft—a much easier and more manageable task than starting cold.

"My daughter is assigned a book a month. She is required to read the book and then take an in-class test based on her reading. She has failed every test.

This month the assigned book is *Johnny Tremain*. She claims that she can't understand the book and wants to rent the video instead."

If the book is extremely difficult for your daughter to read, viewing the video or DVD may enable her to grasp the basic story line. *Watch it with her* well in advance of when the test is scheduled. Then encourage her to read one chapter of the book at a time and discuss it with you. Use the book report outlines on 171–174 to help her study for the test.

"My daughter loves to read but hates to write book reports. She'll talk about a book forever, but writing a report is sheer torture. How can I help make this task more tolerable for her?"

Use the outlines on pages 171–182 to provide structure. Following a format greatly simplifies report writing. If your daughter likes to talk about a book she has just read, encourage her to talk into a recorder while following one of the outlines. When she finishes, she can transcribe her oral report into written form.

"My son would rather read than eat. He reads many more books than required by his teacher, and he writes well-developed book reports. Should I be concerned about his preoccupation with reading?"

Only if he is using reading as a substitute for real-life activities or relationships. If his life is balanced—if he also participates in school activities, plays with friends, and pursues nonbook interests—then celebrate the fact that he has formed such a good habit so early in life.

How to help your child with term papers

Helping your child with a written report may bring flashbacks of your own late nights spent hunched over a typewriter. Grinding out a report at the last minute is nobody's idea of fun. Fortunately, your child can learn from you the benefits of advance planning.

Often children are assigned a report without receiving any instruction on how to go about doing it. Or they may not be taught how to use instruction given previously. For example, children may learn how to outline in a language arts class but may not be shown how to apply this skill to a term paper for a social studies class. Even if they are told what to do, they may never have seen a sample of a finished report. In other words, they may have no idea what is expected of them!

Planning is the key to a successful paper-writing experience. You may have gotten by on all-nighters, but it's your duty as a caring parent to help your child develop healthier habits. With patience and guidance from you, she can develop a far more organized and efficient schedule. The following list of steps can get you started. A checklist you can copy and use is found on pages 183–184.

1. Make sure that your child understands the assignment.

2. Find out all the requirements and specifications for the paper. *Examples:* Will it need a title page? A table of contents? A bibliography? Pictures, illustrations, maps, or other graphics? Should it be typed, or can it be handwritten?

3. Decide on a topic.

4. Have the topic approved by the teacher.

5. Research the topic at the library and/or use home technology resources (CD-ROM encyclopedia, the Internet, and so on). Check the teacher's guidelines for the project; many teachers require that students use various types of resources.

6. Contact community resources related to the topic.

7. Write letters or emails needed to obtain information from national sources.

8. Take notes on the materials found or obtained.

9. Develop an outline.

10. Write a rough draft.

11. Proofread the rough draft using the A-OK method (see pages 69–70).

12. Write the final draft.

Work with your child to set a deadline for each step of this checklist. Decide what she can do independently and where you will need to help. The most difficult steps for children are usually note taking, outlining, and writing the rough draft. A child about to do her first report will probably need a great deal of guidance and support during these steps.

Help!

? **"My daughter, a fourth grader, has been assigned a term paper on** Norway. She did a report on volleyball last month and got a C. Her teacher was upset that she copied from the encyclopedia. Aren't rules about copying material taught later—like in middle school or high school?"

"My son prints out pages he downloads from the Internet and turns these in as term papers. He doesn't understand that this isn't acceptable."

When teachers require children to write reports without giving them any formal instruction on the process to use, parental assistance is much needed. Never write a report for your child, but do help your child to extract information from varied resources and reference materials (including printed materials—books, magazines—and those available through technology resources including CD-ROMs and the Internet) and to paraphrase this information. Help your child learn early on about how to cite another person's work. Plagiarism is a very serious ethical offense at the college level. Students should begin to learn summarization skills and ways to reference the work of others in the intermediate grades.

Give your child a copy of the checklist on pages 183–184 to serve as a guide in planning the project.

Try to make this a positive experience in any way you can. For a daughter assigned a term paper on Norway, you might ask a travel agent for pictures or write to various sources (*example:* the Norwegian Embassy) for information. For a son who loves to surf the Internet, you might encourage him to find several papers or resources on his topic and pull information from all of them into his final report. Or he might post a query in a news group and see what responses come in. (One student I know gathered responses from top scientists around the world.) Your child will be writing reports for a long time, so anything you can do to instill a positive attitude will be extremely important.

 "My son enjoys research and does a fine job of writing term papers for school. What can I do to let him know that I support his efforts—without interfering?"

When your son is researching a topic, let him know that you are interested in what he is doing. Ask him to share his findings at the dinner table. Keep your eyes and ears open for community resources that may enhance his research.

"We should be thrilled that so much technology is available, and we should use whatever we can get our hands on. . . . Don't worry about students becoming dependent on technology. Just be glad it's available to make learning more accessible and exciting for everyone."

SUSAN WINEBRENNER

9

Using Technology

Homework and home computers

Many parents ask whether it's a good idea for their children to use a computer when doing homework. The answer is: It depends. Clearly it's important for children to be comfortable around computers and to know what computers can do—in short, to become computer literate. Making a computer available in the home is an excellent way to facilitate this. But be prepared to exercise some parental control! Excessive use of computers is as bad as too much TV. Children who are always in front of computer monitors don't have time for socializing, reading, or exercise.

If you already own a computer, consider letting your child use it at appropriate

times but not constantly, and provide software that encourages him to study and learn. There are many programs available today that can enliven repetitive drill-and-practice in math, reading, and spelling. They won't necessarily help with Tuesday night's specific homework assignments, but they may sharpen your child's overall skills. And that's a benefit for the long term. You may want to ask your child's teacher about appropriate software so that what you do at home doesn't conflict with what is going on at school.

What if you don't own a home computer? Should you consider buying one? If you can afford one, it would be a good investment, especially if your child is using computers in school. You may opt to purchase a computer that's identical to or compatible with the kind the school has chosen. Check with your child's teacher or the school media center or technology center specialist for specifics.

If a computer isn't in your budget . . .

A home computer may not be in your family budget right now. If that's the case, try the following suggestions to make sure your child has the opportunity to explore the world of computers.

- Some schools have programs that allow parents to borrow a computer for as long as a month at a time. If your school doesn't have such a program, work with the parents' organization to create one.

- Office support centers such as Kinko's and even some cafés have computers available for customers to "rent" on-site. While this might prove expensive over time, it may help you explore word processing systems and decide if a computer is something worth planning and saving for.

- Ask about opportunities at your child's school; perhaps computers in the media or technology center can be used before or after school. Learn what your child is learning with respect to word processing, programming, and use of software programs.

- See if your local public library or media center offers computer use time.

How to decide what software to buy

Computer software can be expensive, the boxes seldom tell you much about the programs inside, and clerks aren't always helpful. Before buying software, it's a good idea to do some research of your own. Several Web sites offer excellent reviews of educational software:

- **SuperKids Educational Software Review** (*www.superkids.com*)

- **EvaluTech** (*www.evalutech.sreb.org*)

- **The Review Zone** (*www.thereviewzone.com*)

- **Viewz Computer Guide** (*www.viewz.com/features/kidcdguide.shtml*)

Other suggestions:

- Your school or local public library might have software you can check out and sample at home.

- Some computer stores allow customers to try software before buying it and also allow boxed programs to be returned within 30 days if customers aren't satisfied with them. (Department and discount stores are less likely to be as liberal with their return policies.)

- You might try previewing games at the homes of your child's friends. And ask other parents what programs they and their children like.

- Consult publications like *Living Digital, Family Computing, Family PC, PC World,* and *Macworld* for previews, reviews, and letters from readers about software programs.

RECOMMENDED CRITERIA FOR CHOOSING SOFTWARE

The best software programs aren't necessarily those with the most awesome technology. Rather, the best programs are those that enhance your child's strengths and interests, just as good books or videos and DVDs can do. Cathy Miranker, coauthor of *The Computer Museum Guide to the Best Software for Kids,* says that software should satisfy the "three Ls": learning, looks, and longevity. Aside from issues of educational soundness (which is sometimes hard for parents to evaluate), smooth functioning, and affordability, the following criteria should help you to decide what software to buy.

Brand name
Although a brand name doesn't guarantee high quality, chances are better than average with publishers with proven track records such as Edmark, the Learning Company, and Maxis. Avoid deeply discounted software, which usually means the programs have done poorly in the marketplace.

Compatibility with home equipment
Jot down your computer's specs (brand, PC or Macintosh, model, RAM, hard drive size, and so on) and carry them with you when shopping. Does a new program require a joystick, more memory, or some other add-on? If so, would it be worth making this purchase for use with additional programs as well?

Ease of use
How long will it take for your child to learn the program? Is her reading level adequate for the program? Can she quit the program for a while and later return quickly to where she left off?

Interest level
Are the audio and visual presentations appealing? Is the program likely to be enjoyable for your child? Does it move speedily enough to hold her interest?

Variety
Is there enough variety in the program that your child will want to return to it again and again?

Skill development
Does the software promote the skills important for today's learners, such as independent thinking, critical thinking, and investigative problem solving?

Challenge
Does the program span a wide range of age and skill levels so your child can grow with it? How long will it take your child to feel a sense of accomplishment from using the program?

Child control
Will your child merely respond to prompts from the program, or will she have an opportunity to create individual pathways toward learning?

Appropriate rewards
Will your child feel that she has created or discovered something after using the software, or is the only "reward" a point value for the number of correct answers? Does feedback include clues? Is the feedback generally supportive and encouraging?

PROGRAMS THAT PROMOTE CRITICAL THINKING AND PROBLEM SOLVING*

Some of the more creative programs on the market build critical thinking and problem-solving skills. Recommended programs include:

- **The Sim Series.** Children and adults engage in exciting simulated problems in *The Sims* and *SimCity* (ages 12 and up). From Maxis.

- **Thinkin' Things Collections.** Collection 1 (ages 4 to 8) strengthens observation, memory, and problem-solving skills while encouraging creativity. Collection 2 (ages 7 to 10) strengthens observation, analysis, spatial awareness, and memory skills and fosters creativity. Collection 3 (ages 8 to 13) improves deductive and inductive reasoning, synthesis, and analysis skills. From Riverdeep.

- *Where in the World Is Carmen Sandiego?* This old favorite for ages 9 and up continues to motivate interest in geography and other cultures. A deluxe edition is enhanced with spectacular sounds and graphics. *Where in the USA Is Carmen Sandiego?* (also for ages 9 and up) is equally good. From Riverdeep.

PROGRAMS THAT TEACH KEYBOARDING

Before children can successfully use a word processing program, they must first learn how to type, or "keyboard." Keyboarding should be taught as soon as children have to enter more than single characters (Y, N, numbers) into the keyboard. Find out if your school provides instruction in keyboarding for your child. If not, you may want to consider providing opportunities to learn keyboarding at home. Some inexpensive programs that teach keyboarding include:

- *JumpStart Typing.* The JumpStart series by Knowledge Adventure teaches keyboarding in an interactive game format. From JumpStart.

- *Mavis Beacon Teaches Typing.* Work at your own pace with lessons that adjust to your age, skill-level, and progress. From Broderbund.

- *Read, Write, and Type.* This software makes a link between reading, writing, keyboarding, and word processing. It has special features for students with learning disabilities and English language learners. From Talking Fingers, Inc.

- *UltraKey.* The strengths of this program lie in its graphics and flexibility. Each lesson supplies information about correct fingering and gives students an opportunity to practice. From Bytes of Learning.

PROGRAMS THAT TEACH WORD PROCESSING

Although all children should learn to compose with a pencil, word processing programs can greatly simplify tasks ranging from vocabulary sentences to book reports. They make it easy to insert or delete

---

*Addresses, telephone numbers, and Web site addresses for the software publishers named in this and the following sections are found on page 122.

sentences, reorganize paragraphs, look up a word in a built-in thesaurus, and correct spelling and grammar. You may need to teach your child the proper use of these tools. *Example:* A spellchecker or grammar-check program may highlight words that are correct or words that your child will have reason to leave "as is." This can be confusing and will require some explanation.

Older children will probably be ready for standard adult word processing programs such as *Word* or *Word Perfect.* For younger students, try:

- *The Ultimate Writing and Creativity Center.* This program helps children (ages 7 to 10) discover the pleasures of seeing their writing in print. From Riverdeep.

C A U T I O N

Check with your child's teacher *before* giving your child permission to do writing assignments on the computer. Some teachers prefer that assignments be handwritten, and younger children especially need practice in this skill. Most teachers prefer that children *not* use spellcheckers.

PROGRAMS THAT REINFORCE BASIC SKILLS

Software may focus on reinforcing specific skills, such as spelling or computation. Or it may simultaneously reinforce several skill areas; in a creative writing program, for example, students might be called on to compose, spell, and punctuate. Following are examples of both types of software:

- **The JumpStart Study Helpers Series.** This series has software for teaching reading, math, spelling, and Spanish. It is highly interactive and seems like a game. From JumpStart.

- *Storybook Weaver Deluxe 2004.* This program motivates children to create their own stories. From Riverdeep.

ENCYCLOPEDIAS ON CD-ROM AND THE INTERNET

CD-ROM and Internet-based encyclopedias bring reference works to life by using digitized pictures, animation, and video clips. Here are several for you to consider:

- *e.encyclopedia.* Appropriate for both elementary and secondary students. This hard book with an enhanced Web site helps to facilitate Internet research. From Dorling Kindersley Publishing.

- *Eyewitness Children's Encyclopedia.* Ages 7 to 11. This multimedia encyclopedia includes more than 5,000 screens and pop-ups, 40 videos, 90 animations, and 2 hours of audio. From Broderbund.

- *Microsoft Encarta Encyclopedia* (encarta.msn.com). A general family reference and research tool for school children. In addition to the encyclopedia, you'll also have access to daily math help, literature guides, researcher tools, paper-writing guides, 60,000+ articles, dictionaries and thesaurus, and an interactive atlas. From Microsoft.

▌Resources

Publishers of Recommended Software

Broderbund • 100 Pine Street, Suite 1900 • San Francisco, CA 94111 • (415) 659-2000 • *www.broderbund.com*

Bytes of Learning Incorporated • 60 Renfrew Drive, Suite 210 • Markham, Ontario, Canada L3R 0E1 • 1-800-465-6428 • *www.bytesoflearning.com*

Dorling Kindersley Publishing • 375 Hudson Street • New York, NY 10014 • 1-800-788-6262 • *us.dk.com*

JumpStart • Vivendi Universal Games • 6080 Center Drive, 10th Floor • Los Angeles, CA 90045 • (310) 431-4000 • *www.jumpstart.com*

Maxis Software • Electronic Arts Inc. • 209 Redwood Shores Parkway • Redwood City, CA 94065 • (650) 628-1500 • *www.maxis.com*

Microsoft Corporation • One Microsoft Way • Redmond, WA 98052 • 1-800-426-9400 • *www.microsoft.com*

Riverdeep Inc. • 100 Pine Street, Suite 1900 • San Francisco, CA 94111 • (415) 659-2000 • *www.riverdeep.com*

Talking Fingers, Inc. • One St. Vincent Drive • San Rafael, CA 94903 • 1-800-674-9126 • *www.talkingfingers.com*

The Internet

The Internet has become a communications tool that knows no boundaries. Not even the lack of a home computer is a problem now that many libraries provide public access. Using a modem connected to a computer, students can talk, research, and share information over telephone lines and on bulletin boards.

You can encourage your child to use the Internet to research information for school projects and for online homework help. If you are just getting started with Internet use, check out these two online resources, which provide suggestions for safe and productive Internet use:

- **"The Parents' Guide to the Information Superhighway"** (*www.childrenspartner ship.org*)

- **"Parents' Guide to the Internet"** (*www.ed.gov/pubs/parents/internet*)

For an online tutorial for parents new to the Internet, check out this site:

- **ParentsPage** (*www.nassaulibrary.org/ parent*)

While the Internet is a wonderful educational tool, it may also expose your child to subjects and images that are inappropriate. For this reason, some parents prefer not to turn their children loose on the Internet. Instead, they choose online services that offer "parental control" features. Others equip their computers with software that claims to block access to questionable areas on the Internet.

C A U T I O N

When children are old enough to use the computer by themselves, have a family meeting to set some guidelines around computer use. Decide how much time your child is allowed to spend on the computer and whether Internet use needs to be supervised. It's wise to keep desktop computers in a central location in your home and to have children use laptops in a location where they can be monitored consistently. Set some family guidelines and stick to them.

It's important to remember that all Internet sites are not created equally. Some are produced by top-notch companies and organizations that carefully review the content of their sites and keep them up-to-date. Other sites, however, do not go though a review process more common in print media. Some sites are even created as hoaxes. Remember, anyone can produce a Web site.

You'll want to help your child—especially older children who are working on school reports—learn how to look at Web sites critically for currency, accuracy, and authenticity. Begin with the following questions:

- What is the date of the Web site? When was the site last updated?

- Does the information seem accurate? Is it consistent with other sources?

- Does the information come from a reliable source? Who created the site? What is the author's name and credentials?

The following two books are also helpful when you are learning how to navigate the Internet:

- *Awesome Internet Sites for Kids* by Sandra Antoniani (Dundas, Ontario: Ride the Wave Media, 2002).

- *How to Find Almost Anything on the Internet: A Kid's Guide to Safe Searching* by Ted Pedersen and Francis Moss (New York: Price Stern Sloan, 2000).

C A U T I O N

While many online services now provide unlimited service for a flat monthly fee, chatlines often charge by the minute. These costs can add up quickly!

World Wide Web sites that can provide hours of fun and learning for your child are appearing at exponential rates. Following is a list of several worth investigating for children ages 8 and above. You can also ask your child's teacher for recommended sites to explore together.

- **A & E Biography Page** (*www.biography. com*). Looking for information about biographies? This site has a database of over 15,000 people.

- **American Library Association** (*www.ala. org/greatsites*). This site is a great starting place for those new to the Internet. The Great Web Sites for Kids section has links to terrific sites in the following categories: animals, literature and language, history and biography, math and computers, social sciences, the arts, and science.

- **The Art Institute of Chicago** (*www.artic. edu/aic*). Can't get to a museum? Many museums have interactive Web pages for children.

- **Ask Jeeves** (*www.ajkids.com*). This is a kid-friendly site that helps users find answers to questions online.

- **Mega Mathematics** (*www.c3.lanl.gov/mega-math*). Interactive projects involving map coloring, graphs, knots, and algorithms, presented by the Los Alamos National Laboratory.

- **MGBnet/Just for Kids** (*mbgnet.mobot.org*). Educational projects linked to kids around the world. The site is sponsored by the Missouri Botanical Garden.

- **Newton's Apple** (*www.ktca.org/newtons*). A supplement to public television's program of the same name, this site features links to lessons on subjects like movie dinosaurs, hang gliding, earthquakes, garlic, and the Internet.

- **Robert Niles' Journalism Help: Finding Data on the Internet** (*www.robertniles.com/data*). Having a hard time finding just what your child needs for a school project? Try this Web site.

- **StarChild: A Learning Center for Young Astronomers** (*starchild.gsfc.nasa.gov/docs/StarChild/ StarChild.html*). A clear, understandable site for learning about space, provided by the High Energy Astrophysics Science Archive Research Center (HEASARC) at NASA.

- **Zoom Inventors and Inventions** (*www.enchantedlearning.com/inventors*). Is your child curious about how things came to be? This site highlights inventions (such as the zipper) and the people who came up with ideas to make life easier and better.

The following Web sites provide links to sites appropriate for children under age 8:

- **Pauline Haass Public Library** (*www.wcfls.lib.wi.us/phpl/preschoolsites. htm*)

- **The University of Connecticut** (*www.literacy.uconn.edu/k2sites.htm*)

The following Web sites provide homework help and links to sites for different subjects and grade levels:

- **About Homework Help** (*www.about.com/homework/index.htm*)

- **Boston Public Library Homework Help** (*www.bpl.org/KIDS/Homework Help.htm*)

- **Discovery School Homework Help & More** (*school.discovery.com/students*)

- **Homework Planet** (*www.homeworkplanet.com*)

- **Homework Spot** (*www.homeworkspot.com*)

- **Yahooligans! The Web Guide for Kids** (*yahooligans.yahoo.com*)

Ethical issues

Technology use has raised many questions of ethics both old and new. Educator David Thornburg has noted that students can create "shovel ware" of their own, pounding out a 300-page tome on virtually any subject by downloading material from the Internet, dressing it up with a few well-chosen images, and pasting on a custom title page. The ethics here are the same as they have always been with research reports: Plagiarism is not scholarship. Following are some tips on ethical issues related to technology use:

- It's *legal* to cut and paste portions of a copyrighted program, such as a video image, into an original presentation; it's *illegal* to present downloaded information verbatim as one's own writing.

- It's *legal* to make one backup copy of a program if it's not included in the original box; it's *illegal* to copy software obtained from another purchaser or to give copies away of software you have purchased.

- It's *legal* to download online freeware or shareware (although shareware authors usually request that you send a small fee).

Help!

"My daughter could use a computer to help with composition homework and with research papers. How do I know what to buy?"

Computers have become more affordable. Making the decision about which computer will work best for your family (for shared use) or for an individual child is very personal. The *Consumer Reports* Web site is a helpful tool for making that decision. The site includes a list of criteria for computer selection (for both desktops and laptops) and reviews of computer hardware currently on the market. Another great feature of this Web site is a glossary of computer terms that is updated regularly.

If you are not knowledgeable in this area, your best bet is to get advice from someone you know and trust. Check with your child's teacher or the technology support person at your child's school for advice.

"How can I control access to the Internet so that my son doesn't come across objectionable material?"

Most Internet service providers now have parental control systems available. Take the time to set the controls as you see appropriate. However, there is virtually no way to prevent a bright, determined child from finding something he really wants to see. And sometimes objectionable material is inadvertently viewed. Search engines often bring up objectionable sites with seemingly innocuous searches. The best way to control your child's access to the Internet is by supervising and monitoring your child's time online, setting firm limitations, establishing clear rules for use, and also establishing (and enforcing) reasonable consequences for violating those rules. Also discuss what your child should do if he inadvertently comes across obscene material on the Internet.

> *"We learn simply by the exposure of living. Much that passes for education is not education at all but ritual. The fact is that we are being educated when we know it least."*
>
> DAVID P. GARDNER

10

Playing Games

The value of playing games with your child

A friend of mine grew up with five brothers and sisters. The expense of raising so many children left little money for movies and other "going-out" activities. Instead, her parents made sure that the house was stocked with games of all kinds—and all of the children grew up to be avid game players. Although the primary intent may not have been educational, the end results certainly were. My friend recalls learning how to spell over a *Scrabble* board, learning about money playing *Monopoly*, and developing other important skills while gathered around the table with her family.

The main reason to play games with your child is because it's *fun*. It's a wonderful opportunity for you to spend time together doing something you both enjoy. It's also a ready-made opportunity for you to reinforce basic concepts and skills. In the context of doing homework, games can provide relief from the monotony and drudgery of drill-and-practice. (Almost any child would rather play Hangman than review a written spelling list.) This chapter includes suggestions for dozens of games you can buy or make yourself.* Many can be used to help teach a variety of subjects.

---

*See also the descriptions of recommended software in Chapter 9. Many of these programs use a game format.

"And the winner is . . ."

While recent years have seen the introduction of many noncompetitive games (games where "everyone wins"), most are still designed to have one person emerge as the winner. When you first play a game with your child that's new to him, it's almost a given that you will be the winner. Parents often wonder whether they should deliberately "lose" on occasion so their children won't be frustrated. Although this desire is understandable, doing so is really not recommended. All children would rather win than lose, but most can tell the difference between *really* winning and winning because someone lets them. Instead, try these strategies for leveling the playing field:

1. When playing a game with your child, keep the focus on *self-competition*. Encourage your child to improve his level of achievement each time the game is played. (For example, your child could aim for a higher personal score or a faster time.)

2. Explore several different types of games with your child. Look for one or more that he can eventually play well enough to win. (It's more fun for you when your child reaches this point.) You may find that your child has a gift for certain games; I know one third grader who was beating his father at chess by age six.

3. Don't limit your choices to games of skill. Also include games of chance, where your child has the same likelihood of winning as you do. Young children enjoy *Candyland, Chutes and Ladders,* and other games where moves are determined by a card, spinner, or a roll of the dice. These may not be appropriate for homework sessions, since they don't teach much in the way of concepts or skills, but they are fine for other occasions. They do teach social skills, such as taking turns and following a set of rules.

When to play games with your child

Naturally you can play games during leisure time "just for the fun of it," but games can also be incorporated into regular homework sessions. For example, instead of doing multiplication flash cards, play Multiplication Baseball. Draw a baseball field and let your child go from base to base with each fact she gets right. Points are scored for each run.

In most cases, games should be scheduled for the end of a homework session. ("When you finish all of your other work— neatly and completely—we'll play a game together.") The game can function as the "carrot" at the end of the homework "stick."

If your child is a slow worker, this may not be the best approach. Many teachers permit students to play learning games only after their regular class work is finished. A child who can't get everything done in time feels left out of the fun. You probably can't change the teacher's policy about this, but you can make up for it at home. Divide your child's homework into mini-sessions and play games in between.

Use games frequently to provide the extra drill needed to overlearn information for a test. Children don't mind going over facts again and again if it involves an element of play. (At least, they don't mind as much.)

How to buy games to play with your child

Many commercial games are available through educational suppliers as well as regular toy stores, department stores, and catalogs. Their quality varies greatly. Be sure to examine a game carefully *before* purchasing it. You may not be able to open it in the store, but directions are usually printed on the bottom of the box, and you can use these to determine whether a game is appropriate for your child's needs and skill level. Inquire about the company's return/refund policy at the time of purchase in case a particular game doesn't work out. Here are 12 more questions to guide your buying decision:

1. Does this game reinforce a specific skill or skills my child needs to master?

2. Do I have the time to make an inexpensive game that will do the job as effectively? (If so, stop here and give it a try. If not, continue.)

3. Is the game attractive and appealing in theme, color, and design?

4. Is the game well-constructed and durable?

5. Is the skill level appropriate for my child? (Most games indicate an age level— for example, "for ages five and up"—but this won't necessarily conform to your child's *skill* level. So this question will take some thought.)

6. Are the directions clear and easy to follow?

7. How long does it take to complete the game? Is it too long or too short to fit the time period I have in mind?

8. How much actual drill-and-practice does the game involve? (Some supposedly "educational" games contain a lot of nonsense or distracting filler activities. These are okay for leisure play but not for homework sessions.)

9. Does the game enable a child to gauge his own progress in skill development? For example, with a trivia game, a child will know when he is improving.

10. Can the entire game, or parts of the game, be adapted for uses other than those specified by the manufacturer?

11. Is the game simple enough that my child can play it with siblings or friends and without a great deal of help from me?

And, finally:

12. Taking all of these factors into consideration, is the game worth the cost?

As you search store shelves and catalog pages for games appropriate for your child, you may feel overwhelmed by the sheer number of games available. Following are some tried-and-true favorites and newer games that come recommended by parents and children alike. See page 130 for manufacturers' addresses in the event that you can't find these games in stores.*

---

*Many of the games listed here—including *Monopoly, Yahtzee, Mille Bornes, Scrabble,* chess, and checkers—are also available in versions for home computers.

- **Addition:** *Yahtzee* (Milton Bradley); *SMATH* (Pressman); *Mille Bornes* (Winning Moves)

- **Making change:** *Monopoly* (Parker Brothers)

- **Spelling and vocabulary:** *Boggle* (Parker Brothers); *Junior Scrabble* (Milton Bradley); *Wheel of Fortune* (Pressman); *UpWords* (Milton Bradley)

- **Classification:** *Pyramid* (Endless Games)

- **General information:** *Go to the Head of the Class* (Winning Moves); *ASAP, Brain Quest, 20 Questions for Kids,* and *Game of Knowledge* (all University Games); *Outburst* (Get Together)

- **Science:** *Mars 2020* (Aristoplay); *Totally Gross—The Game of Science* (University Games)

- **Geography:** *Risk* (Parker Brothers)

- **Strategic thinking:** checkers, chess, Chinese checkers

When playing these games—and any others you choose—it's important to let your child participate in as many ways as possible. It may seem easier or more efficient for you to keep score or make change, but in the long run, your child will benefit more if you let him assume these responsibilities.

▌Resources

Manufacturers of Recommended Games

If you can't find games of interest in stores or catalogs, write to or call the manufacturers. (When you contact them, request a catalog; you may find descriptions of other games worth considering now or in the future.) In some cases, you can order directly from the manufacturer (after requesting ordering information). In other cases, companies will refer you to stores in your area that carry their products.

- **Aristoplay, Ltd.** • 901 Lincoln Parkway • Plainwell, MI 49080 • 1-800-433-4263 • *www.aristoplay.com*

- **Endless Games** • 620 Newark Avenue, Second Floor • Jersey City, NJ 07306 • (201) 386-9465 • *www.endlessgames.com*

- **Get Together Games, Milton Bradley, Parker Brothers** • Hasbro, Inc. • 1027 Newport Avenue • Pawtucket, RI 02861 • 1-888-836-7025 • *www.hasbro.com*

- **Pressman Toy Corporation** • 745 Joyce Kilmer Avenue • New Brunswick, NJ 08901 • 1-800-800-0298 • *www.pressmantoy.com*

- **University Games Corporate** • 2030 Harrison Street • San Francisco, CA 94110 • (415) 503-1600 • *www.ugames.com*

- **Winning Moves Games, Inc.** • 100 Conifer Hill Road, Suite 102 • Danvers, MA 01923 • 1-800-664-7788 • *www.winning-moves.com*

Games you can make at home

When the cost of a commercial game is prohibitive or unwarranted, when a commercial game is not readily available for a specific skill your child needs to master, or when you decide at the spur of the moment that an educational game would liven up a homework session—then make one yourself! Here are some general guidelines for creating homemade learning games:

1. Don't spend more time making the game than your child will spend playing it. (Depending on the skill it's intended to teach, you may only need to use it once or twice.)

2. Have a specific learning goal in mind. Don't try to incorporate too many goals into one game.

3. Get your child involved in the game-making process. You may want to turn this into a problem-solving activity. ("Let's see, you need to study your states and capitals. How can we make a game of it?")

4. Brainstorm together an imaginative name or theme for the game.

5. Have plenty of materials on hand—scissors, construction paper, cardboard, markers, rulers, and so on. If neither you nor your child is artistically inclined, use magazine, comic book, or coloring book pictures to decorate the game. Stickers and rubber stamps are other creative possibilities.

6. *Write down the rules.* Not only does this avoid future conflict; it also models a writing activity for your child.

7. Don't feel as if you have to make game cards for each and every game. For example, if your child needs to prepare for a science test, just use the questions at the end of the chapter or make up questions based on the text. If your child needs to drill on

math problems or reading exercises, use the problems or exercises from the text.

8. Store all learning games and game pieces in your child's study center. Use a plastic dishwashing tub, a milk crate, a tote bag, or a special shelf for keeping odds and ends together.

RECOMMENDED GAME FORMATS AND SUGGESTED WAYS TO PLAY

This section provides some "generic" game formats you can adapt to your child's interests and tailor to skills that need reinforcing. Use your imagination (and your child's) to build these into enjoyable games that meet educational goals. These formats are appropriate for elementary children of all ages; the level of difficulty for each game depends on the content.

Also suggested are several ways to use each game format to teach or reinforce specific skills. Many of these suggestions are interchangeable from one format to another.

Finally, sample "cards" or "boards" for some of the games are provided on pages 185–187. You might make copies of several of these, then have them laminated (or cover them with clear contact paper) so they can be written on with erasable crayon and used several times. Naturally, you can also use paper and pencil or chalkboard and chalk for most of these games.

BINGO
Materials needed:

- poker chips, or other space markers
- traditional Bingo cards (see page 185)
- bingo numbers

Rules of play:

1. Call out a question or flash a flash card.

2. If your child provides the correct response, draw a Bingo number, call it out, and have her put a marker on the corresponding space.

3. Play continues until your child gets "BINGO"—five markers in a row either horizontally, vertically, or diagonally.

Ways to play:

- Learning letters: Write lowercase letters on the Bingo card. Make flash cards of corresponding uppercase letters. (Or do this the other way around.) Show your child a flash card and ask her to match it to a letter on the Bingo board. *Variation:* Have your child match cursive with manuscript letters.

- Learning vowels: Label the five columns on the board with A-E-I-O-U rather than B-I-N-G-O. Call out a word. If your child correctly identifies the vowel sound, she may place a marker in any square in that vowel column.

- Learning sight words: Write vocabulary words in the squares on the Bingo board. Read them aloud, one at a time, and have your child cover each word she recognizes.

- Learning math facts: Write numerals and math symbols in the squares on the Bingo card. Call out the numbers or symbols ("one," "plus," "divided by") and have your child cover each one she recognizes.

- Studying science or social studies questions: Write answers on the Bingo board. Read the questions and have your child cover each match.

- Learning states and capitals: Call out a capital. If your child correctly names the state, draw a BINGO number card and have her cover the corresponding square on the card. (Or do this the other way around: You name the state, and she names the capital.)

TIC-TAC-TOE

Materials needed:

- tic-tac-toe board (see page 186)
- pen or pencil

Rules of play:

1. Your child is "X" and you're "O."

2. Ask your child a question. If he answers it correctly, he marks an "X" on the board. If he answers it incorrectly, you mark an "O" on the board.

3. Play continues until one of you gets "Tic-Tac-Toe"—three Xs or Os in a row, either horizontally, vertically, or diagonally.

Ways to play:

- Learning vocabulary: Have your child define vocabulary terms.

- Learning grammar: Have your child complete an item in a grammar exercise (*example:* locate a subject or verb in a sentence).

- Learning to count: "Skip count" by 2s, 3s, or 4s (or some other number) up to a certain number; then have your child give the next number in the sequence.

- Learning to spell: Dictate a spelling word; then have your child write it correctly.

DOTS GAME

Materials needed:

- dots board (see page 187)
- marker

Rules of play:

1. Explain that the object of the game is to make squares by joining dots with horizontal and vertical lines.

2. Ask your child a question. If she answers it correctly, she draws a line on the board. If she answers it incorrectly, you draw a line on the board.

3. When a square is completed, the player initials the box and immediately gets another turn.

4. When all squares on the board have been completed, the player with the most initialed squares wins.

Ways to play:

- Learning consonants: Read a word out loud. Have your child identify the beginning or ending consonant sound.

- Learning prefixes or suffixes: Show your child a word written on a flash card. Have her identify the prefix or suffix.

- Learning capitalization and punctuation: Show your child a sentence with a capitalization or punctuation error. Have her identify the error and explain how it should be corrected.

- Learning Roman numerals: Show your child Roman numerals written on flash cards and have her identify them.

- Learning to read maps or graphics: Ask questions about maps or graphics you show to your child.

CONCENTRATION

Materials needed:

- Homemade flash cards or playing cards with word or math problems written on one side. Each card must have a match—either a duplicate of the problem or the answer to the problem. The difficulty of the game will depend on the problems themselves and the number of cards.

Rules of play:

1. Shuffle the cards; then lay them out one deep and upside-down in a square or a rectangle.

2. To take a turn, a player turns over any two cards.

3. If the cards match, the player removes them from the board and immediately gets another turn.

4. If the cards don't match, the card are placed back upside-down and the next player takes a turn.

5. Play continues until all matches have been made. The player with the most matches wins.

Ways to play:

- Learning sight words: Make card sets using vocabulary words. Have your child say the word out loud when he finds a match.

- Learning synonyms *(big-large),* antonyms *(big-small),* and homonyms *(blue-blew):* Make card sets using these kinds of words.

- Learning math facts: Make card sets of math problems having the same answer *(examples:* 1 + 5 and 4 + 2, or 6 × 2 and 3 × 4).

- Learning the parts of speech: Make card sets of examples and definitions.

- Learning map symbols: Make card sets of map symbols or abbreviations and definitions.

CARD GAMES

Materials needed:

- Homemade playing cards with words or math problems on one side. Each card must have a match—either a duplicate of the problem or the answer to the problem.

Rules of play:

1. Follow the rules for Go Fish or Wet Cat (played the same as Old Maid).

2. In the case of Wet Cat, a wild card will be needed.

Ways to play:

You can use your homemade cards to help your child learn the following (among other ideas of your own):

- rhyming words
- the halves of compound words
- vocabulary words and definitions
- words and their abbreviations
- Arabic and Roman numerals

HANGMAN

Materials needed:

- paper and pencil or chalkboard and chalk

Rules of play:

1. Explain that the object of the game is to identify an unknown word, starting with only the number of letters.

2. Think of a word; then draw a space for each letter on the paper or chalkboard.

3. Have your child guess one letter at a time. If the letter is included in the "mystery word," write it in the appropriate blank space (or spaces). If the letter is not included in the word, draw a body part in the Hangman. *(Hint:* It's wise to agree ahead of time on which body parts should be included. Sometimes, in an attempt to win, children will want everything to count, from eyelashes to toenails.)

4. To win, your child must identify the mystery word before all of the Hangman's body parts are drawn.

Ways to play:

- Learning spelling words: Work from your child's test list for that week, and include review words from past weeks.

- Learning vocabulary words: Have your child give the definition of the word after identifying it.

- Learning names of cities, states, and/or countries: Work from the chapters your child is studying in her social studies text, and include review names from past weeks.

MATCH-UPS

Several different formats can be used for matching games. Each requires a different set of materials, but all share the same rules and applications.

Matching Wheel:

1. Cut out a 14-inch circular piece of cardboard and draw lines dividing it into "pie pieces."

2. Cover the cardboard with clear contact paper.

3. Use erasable crayon to label each pie piece with one-half of a match.

4. Use sticky notes or clothespins to create the other halves of the matches.

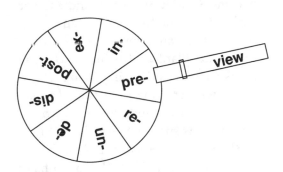

Matching Mini-Puzzles:

1. Write one-half of a match on each side of an index card.

2. Cut the card into two interlocking pieces.

Homemade Dominoes:

1. Divide 2" x 4" pieces of tagboard in two by drawing a line down the middle of each one.

2. On each half, draw a word, symbol, or number.

3. Make sure that each word, symbol, or number is paired with itself at least once and paired with every other word, symbol, or number in the set at least once. Also make sure to include some blanks. Here's an example of what part of a set might look like:

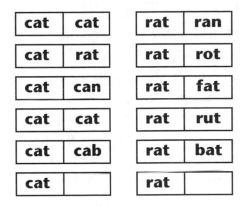

cat	cat		rat	ran
cat	rat		rat	rot
cat	can		rat	fat
cat	cat		rat	rut
cat	cab		rat	bat
cat			rat	

Rules of play, all match-up games:

1. Explain that the object of the game is to make all the matches correctly, reading them as they are made.

2. To add an element of excitement, have your child do this under timed conditions and try to better his time with each round.

Ways to play:

The possibilities for match-up games are virtually limitless. Types of matches might include:

- words and pictures representing the words

- prefixes or suffixes and root words

- names of land forms ("plateau," "peninsula") or bodies of water ("lake," "inlet") and diagrams or descriptions

- sentences with missing vocabulary words and the vocabulary words

- numerals and corresponding numbers of dots

- states and abbreviations

- measurement abbreviations and identifications

SORTING GAMES

Materials needed:

- small slips of paper labeled with the names, problems, definitions, questions, and so on, to be sorted

- shoe boxes or small paper lunch bags, labeled and used as containers (for sorting only a few categories)

- egg cartons (for sorting up to 12 different categories)

Rules of play:

1. Explain that the object of the game is to sort the items correctly into categories.

2. To add an element of excitement, have your child do this under timed conditions and try to better her time with each round.

Ways to play:

The possibilities for sorting games are virtually limitless. Categories might include:

- long and short vowel sounds

- hard and soft "g" and "c" words (*go* and *age, cat* and *face*)

- true and false statements

- animals (vertebrates or invertebrates, warm-blooded or cold-blooded)

- singular and plural nouns

MAKING YOUR OWN BOARD GAMES

You don't have to make board games from scratch to create ones that meet your goals for your child. You can use games you already have if you tie taking turns to answering questions, reading vocabulary words, or solving math problems. It's easy to design your own Reading Pursuit, Math Pursuit, Spelling Pursuit, Social Studies Pursuit, or whatever. If you don't have any board games that you think will work for these purposes, here are some ideas to try:

- Folders are great for board games. If the folder has a picture on the outside, it can help determine the theme of the game. For example, a folder with a baseball pitcher on the front can become Syllable Strikeout, and a folder with cats on the front cover can become Capitalization Cat-Nap. Most folders are blank on the inside. Use this blank surface as the game board. Draw a path with crayon or felt-tipped pens, and be sure to include squares with instructions such as *Start, Go Back (1, 2, 3) Spaces, Go Forward (1, 2, 3) Spaces, Free Turn,* and *Finish.* If the folder has a pocket, use it for storing place markers, rules, game pieces, score pads, and other materials used to play the game.

- If your child is a sports fan, draw a football, soccer, or baseball field instead of a regular game board pathway. Your child earns "yardage," "goals," or "base hits" with every correct answer.

- Instead of making a traditional square or rectangular game board, cut out the shape of a favorite cartoon character;

a musical instrument; a state, country, or continent; a car or locomotive; and so on.

- Science board games can be especially interesting. The path you draw might wind through the human circulatory or digestive system, the solar system, or layers of the earth (from core to crust)—with these serving as the game themes.

- Real road maps make excellent game boards, and your child can learn map-reading skills simultaneously. If your child is studying a country or a continent in social studies, try to find a corresponding map. Use a felt-tipped pen to draw a pathway between major locations on a city, state, or country map.

- Instead of a board, why not use a yard-stick or meterstick? With each correct answer, your child can move the marker (a slider or a rubber band) an inch or a decimeter.

You can use homemade board games to test almost anything—from sight words to math facts, spelling words to scientific concepts.

"Education is too important to be left solely to the educators."

FRANCIS KEPPEL

More Resources and Tools You Can Use

Recommended reading

Checking Your Grammar by Marvin Terban (New York: Scholastic, 1994). This kids' manual of style covers spelling rules, punctuation, capitalization, contractions, parts of speech, abbreviations, acronyms, and the 100 most often confused and misused words. The author has also written: *Verbs, Verbs, Verbs; Building Your Vocabulary; Punctuation Power;* and *Scholastic Dictionary of Idioms,* among others.

Choosing Books for Children: A Commonsense Guide by Betsy Hearne with Deborah Stevenson (Champaign, IL: University of Illinois Press, 2000). Chapters are devoted to selecting different types of books; over 100 titles are recommended.

Classics to Read Aloud to Your Children by William Russell (New York: Crown, 1992). Each selection indicates the age of the child it's suited for and offers suggestions for making a read-aloud session enjoyable. Also by the author is *Classic Myths to Read Aloud: The Great Stories of Greek and Roman Mythology, Specially Arranged for Children Five and Up.*

For Reading Out Loud! by Margaret M. Kimmel and Elizabeth Segal (New York: Dell, 1991). Explains why it's important to read aloud all through the childhood years, tells how to make time to do it, and gives effective ways of reading over 140 suggested books.

The Read-Aloud Handbook by Jim Trelease (New York: Penguin Books, 2001). Discusses the hows and whys of reading aloud; contains over 300 annotated read-aloud selections.

Scholastic Homework Reference Series: Desk References for Students and Parents by Anne Zeman and Kate Kelly (New York: Scholastic). Includes *Everything You Need to Know About American History Homework* (1995), . . . *Math Homework* (1994), . . . *Science Homework* (2005), . . . *English Homework* (1995), . . . *Geography Homework* (1997), and . . . *World History Homework* (1995).

School Power: Study Skill Strategies for Succeeding in School by Jeanne S. Schumm (Minneapolis: Free Spirit Publishing, 2001). Covers everything students need to know, from how to get organized to how to take notes, study smarter, write better, follow directions, handle homework, manage long-term assignments, and more.

Seven Pathways of Learning: Teaching Students and Parents About Multiple Intelligences by David Lazear (Tucson: Zephyr Press, 1994). Ways to help young people tap into their full learning potential and enrich their lifelong learning in and out of school.

Stand Up for Your Gifted Child: How to Make the Most of Kids' Strengths at School and at Home by Joan Franklin Smutny (Minneapolis: Free Spirit Publishing, 2001). Learn how to recognize and understand your child's gifts, explore options available to your child from the school, and provide learning enrichment at home.

You're Smarter Than You Think: A Kid's Guide to Multiple Intelligences by Thomas Armstrong (Minneapolis: Free Spirit Publishing, 2003). Based on Howard Gardner's theory of multiple intelligences, this book explains the eight intelligences in a language kids can understand, helps them identify their own strengths, and shows them how to build the other intelligences.

Your Child Can Read Better: A Handbook for Parents by Donna Hartmann and Arlyss Stump (Holmes Beach, FL: Learning Publications, 1980). Background information about reading, with after-school and summer reading activities, games, and gift ideas.

The **International Reading Association** offers several brochures for parents that can be downloaded for free at *www.reading.org/resources/tools/parent.html*. Or send a self-addressed, stamped envelope to 800 Barksdale Road, Newark, DE 19714, for a free copy:

- Explore the Playground of Books: Tips for Parents of Beginning Readers

- Family Literacy and the School Community: A Partnership for Lifelong Learning

- Get Ready to Read! Tips for Parents of Young Children

- Good Nutrition Leads to Better Learning

- Library Safari: Tips for Parents of Young Readers and Explorers

- Make the Reading-Writing Connection: Tips for Parents of Young Learners

- Making the Most of Television: Tips for Parents of Young Viewers

- Prepare Your Child for Reading Tests

- See the World on the Internet: Tips for Parents of Young Readers—and "Surfers"

- Summer Reading Adventure! Tips for Parents of Young Readers

- Understanding Your Child's Learning Differences

- What Is Family Literacy? Getting Involved in Your Child's Literacy Learning

Organizations

The following organizations are excellent sources of information for parents as well as teachers.

- **American Library Association** • 50 East Huron Street • Chicago, IL 60611 • 1-800-545-2433 • *www.ala.org*

- **International Reading Association** • 800 Barksdale Road • Newark, DE 19714 • 1-800-336-7323 • *www.reading.org*

- **National Council of Teachers of English** (NCTE) • 1111 West Kenyon Road • Urbana, IL 61801 • (217) 328-3870 • *www.ncte.org*

- **National Council of Teachers of Mathematics** (NCTM) • 1906 Association Drive • Reston, VA 20191 • (703) 620-9840 • *www.nctm.org*

NCTM is primarily an association for educators, but it's worth checking into some of their publications. See especially *Curriculum and Evaluation Standards for School Mathematics*, which helps to explain why teachers may be teaching the way they are.

- **Reading Is Fundamental, Inc.** • 1825 Connecticut Avenue NW, Suite 400 • Washington, DC 20009 • 1-877-743-7323 • *www.rif.org*

   Articles for parents such as "Building a Family Library," "Encouraging Young Writers," "Reading Aloud to Your Children," "Helping Kids Adjust to School: Useful Tips for Parents and Educators," "Helping with Homework," and many more are available online.

Tools

On the following pages, you'll find forms, lists, charts, game boards, and more that you can use to help your child with homework. Suggestions for using them are included throughout the book, but don't limit yourself to these ideas. You may find that some of these tools can serve several purposes.

   Alternate versions of some of the forms are included. Let your child choose the one she likes best.

Certificate of Congratulations!

TO

_____

FOR SUCCESSFULLY COMPLETING

_____

_____   _____

SIGNED   DATE

Date _____

Certificate of Congratulations

To

_____

For successfully completing

_____

Good Job!

_____

Signed

Assignment
Sheet

WEEK OF: _____

DATE OF ASSIGNMENT	SUBJECT	BOOK OR PROJECT	PAGE(S)	DATE DUE	GRADE

ASSIGNMENT SHEET

WEEK OF

DATE OF ASSIGNMENT	SUBJECT	BOOK OR PROJECT	PAGE(S)	DATE DUE	GRADE

The Instant (Sight) Words*

The First 100 Words (approximately first grade)

Group 1a	Group 1b	Group 1c	Group 1d
the	he	go	who
a	I	see	an
is	they	then	their
you	one	us	she
to	good	no	new
and	me	him	said
we	about	by	did
that	had	was	boy
in	if	come	three
not	some	get	down
for	up	or	work
at	her	two	put
with	do	man	were
it	when	little	before
on	so	has	just
can	my	them	long
will	very	how	here
are	all	like	other
of	would	our	old
this	any	what	take
your	been	know	cat
as	out	make	again
but	there	which	give
be	from	much	after
have	day	his	many

The Instant (Sight) Words*

The Second 100 Words (approximately second grade)

Group 2a	Group 2b	Group 2c	Group 2d
saw	big	may	ran
home	where	let	five
soon	am	use	read
stand	ball	these	over
box	morning	right	such
upon	live	present	way
first	four	tell	too
came	last	next	shall
girl	color	please	own
house	away	leave	most
find	red	hand	sure
because	friend	more	thing
made	pretty	why	only
could	eat	better	near
book	want	under	than
look	year	while	open
mother	white	should	kind
run	got	never	must
school	play	each	high
people	found	best	far
night	left	another	both
into	men	seem	end
say	bring	tree	also
think	wish	name	until
back	black	dear	call

*The Instant (Sight) Words are reprinted with permission of Edward Fry, Ph.D., Laguna Beach Educational Books. From *How to Help Your Child with Homework* by Jeanne Shay Schumm, Ph.D., copyright © 2005. Free Spirit Publishing Inc., Minneapolis, MN; 866/703-7322; *www.freespirit.com*. This page may be photocopied for individual, classroom, and small group work only.

The Instant (Sight) Words*

The Third 100 Words (approximately third grade)

Group 3a	Group 3b	Group 3c	Group 3d
ask	hat	off	fire
small	car	sister	ten
yellow	write	happy	order
show	try	once	part
goes	myself	didn't	early
clean	longer	set	fat
buy	those	round	third
thank	hold	dress	same
sleep	full	fell	love
letter	carry	wash	hear
jump	eight	start	yesterday
help	sing	always	eyes
fly	warm	anything	door
don't	sit	around	clothes
fast	dog	close	through
cold	ride	walk	o'clock
today	hot	money	second
does	grow	turn	water
face	cut	might	town
green	seven	hard	took
every	woman	along	pair
brown	funny	bed	now
coat	yes	fine	keep
six	ate	sat	head
gave	stop	hope	food

The Instant (Sight) Words*

The Second 300 Words (approximately fourth grade)

Group 4a	Group 4b	Group 4c	Group 4d
told	time	word	wear
Miss	yet	almost	Mr.
father	true	thought	side
children	above	send	poor
land	still	receive	lost
interest	meet	pay	outside
government	since	nothing	wind
feet	number	need	Mrs.
garden	state	mean	learn
done	matter	late	held
country	line	half	front
different	remember	fight	built
bad	large	enough	family
across	few	feel	began
yard	hit	during	air
winter	cover	gone	young
table	window	hundred	ago
story	even	week	world
sometimes	city	between	airplane
I'm	together	change	without
tried	sun	being	kill
horse	life	care	ready
something	street	answer	stay
brought	party	course	won't
shoes	suit	against	paper

(1 of 3: continues)

The Instant (Sight) Words*

The Second 300 Words (continued)

Group 4e	Group 4f	Group 4g	Group 4h
hour	grade	egg	spell
glad	brother	ground	beautiful
follow	remain	afternoon	sick
company	milk	feed	became
believe	several	boat	cry
begin	war	plan	finish
mind	able	question	catch
pass	charge	fish	floor
reach	either	return	stick
month	less	sir	great
point	train	fell	guess
rest	cost	hill	bridges
sent	evening	wood	church
talk	note	add	lady
went	past	ice	tomorrow
bank	room	chair	snow
ship	flew	watch	whom
business	office	alone	women
whole	cow	how	among
short	visit	arm	road
certain	wait	dinner	farm
fair	teacher	hair	cousin
reason	spring	service	bread
summer	picture	class	wrong
fill	bird	quite	age

(2 of 3: continues)

The Instant (Sight) Words*

The Second 300 Words (continued)

Group 4i	Group 4j	Group 4k	Group 4l
become	herself	demand	aunt
body	idea	however	system
chance	drop	figure	lie
act	river	case	cause
die	smile	increase	marry
real	son	enjoy	possible
speak	bat	rather	supply
already	fact	sound	thousand
doctor	sort	eleven	pen
step	king	music	condition
itself	dark	human	perhaps
nine	themselves	court	produce
baby	whose	force	twelve
minute	study	plant	rode
ring	fear	suppose	uncle
wrote	move	law	labor
happen	stood	husband	public
appear	himself	moment	consider
heart	strong	person	thus
swim	knew	result	least
felt	often	continue	power
fourth	toward	price	mark
I'll	wonder	serve	president
kept	twenty	national	voice
well	important	wife	whether

(3 of 3)

STORY STUDY GUIDE

Title: _____

Author: _____

ABOUT THE SETTING

Time: _____

Place: _____

ABOUT THE CHARACTERS

_____

_____

_____

_____

_____

_____

_____ *(continues)*

STORY STUDY GUIDE
(CONTINUED)

ABOUT THE STORY

The major problem in the story: _____

_____

_____

How the problem was resolved: _____

_____

_____

ABOUT THE PLOT

_____

_____

_____

_____

VOCABULARY

Identify and define the most difficult words in the story.

_____

_____

_____

_____

Story
Study
Guide

Title: _____

Author: _____

About the Setting

Time: _____

Place: _____

About the Characters

List names and nicknames, physical descriptions, and personality descriptions.

_____

_____

_____

_____

_____

_____

_____

_____

_____

_____ *(continues)*

Story Study Guide

About the Story

The major problem in the story: _____

_____

_____

How the problem was resolved: _____

_____

_____

About the Plot

List five major events in the story.

_____

_____

_____

_____

_____

Vocabulary

Identify and define the most difficult words in the story.

_____

_____

Guide for
Story Reading

Step 1: Get Ready

- **Read the title page.**
- **Skim through the book looking at illustrations.**
- **Answer these questions:**

What is the title of the story? _____

Who is the author of the story? _____

Who is the illustrator of the story? _____

What is the setting of the story? _____

    Time in history: _____

    Place: _____

What do I predict this story will be about? _____

Step 2: Get Set

- **Read the first few pages or first chapter.**
- **Identify the main characters in the story.**
- **Answer these questions:**

Who are the main characters in the story? _____

_____

_____

What do I know about these characters? _____

_____

_____

_____

_____ **(continues)**

Guide for
Story Reading (continued)

Step 3: Go

• **Read the rest of the story or the next chapter.**

• **Stop from time to time while reading to summarize what is going on and how you react to the story.**

Step 4: Cool Down

• **Think about what you read.**

• **Answer these questions:**

What were the key events in this story? _____

_____

_____

What part of the story did I like best? _____

_____

_____

What part of the story did I like least? _____

_____

_____

Would I recommend this story to a friend? Why or why not? _____

_____

_____

Step 5: Follow Up

• **List ideas about how you could learn more about the topic discussed in this book.**

_____

_____

Guide for Reading Informational Text

Reading assignment: _____

Topic: _____

Step 1: Preview

- **Look at the pictures, charts, and graphs.**

- **Quickly read the introduction, headings, subheadings, and summary.**

- **Answer these questions:**

  What do I know about this topic? _____

  _____

  What do I think I'm going to learn about this topic? _____

  _____

Step 2: Action Reading

- **Read the assignment, one section at a time.**

- **After each section, identify and fix up "clunks" (difficult or confusing words or ideas).**

- **List two or three key ideas from the section.**

  Section 1:

  Clunks: _____

  Key Ideas: _____

  Section 2:

  Clunks: _____

  Key Ideas: _____

(continues)

Guide for Reading Informational Text (continued)

Section 3:

Clunks: _____

Key Ideas: _____

Section 4:

Clunks: _____

Key Ideas: _____

Step 3: Wrap-up

• **Think about the whole passage you read.**

• **Talk about the most important ideas.**

Most important ideas: _____

_____

_____

_____

_____

_____

_____

• **Predict five or six questions the teacher might ask on a test.**

_____

_____

_____

_____

_____

_____

Manuscript Chart
Zaner-Bloser Style

Manuscript Practice Paper

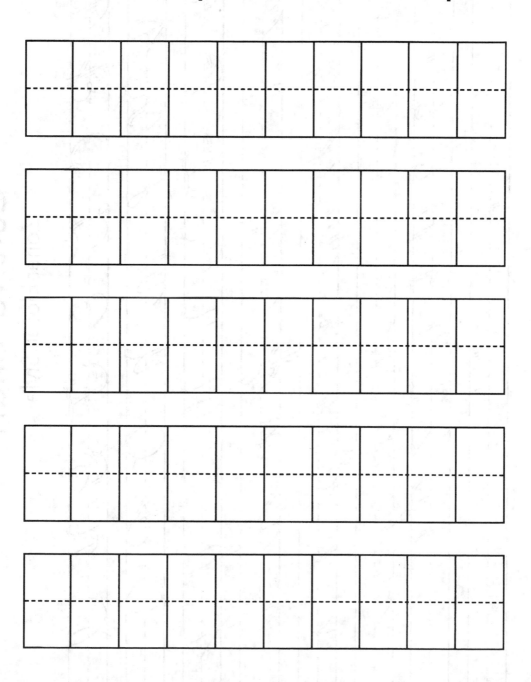

Cursive Chart
Zaner-Bloser Style

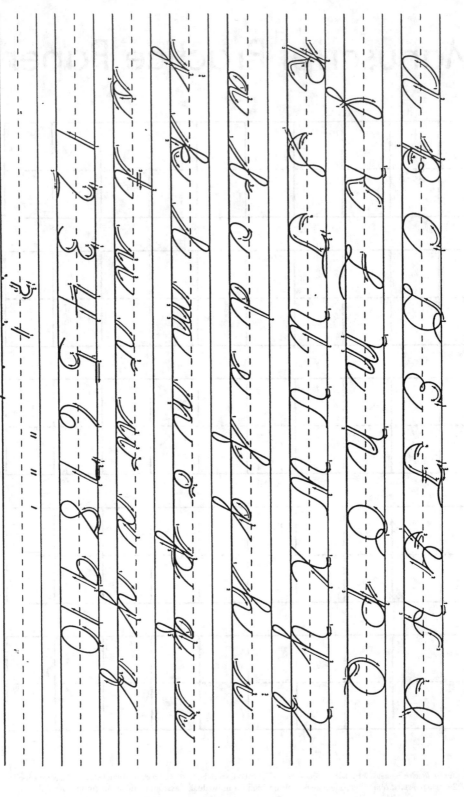

Cursive Practice Sample

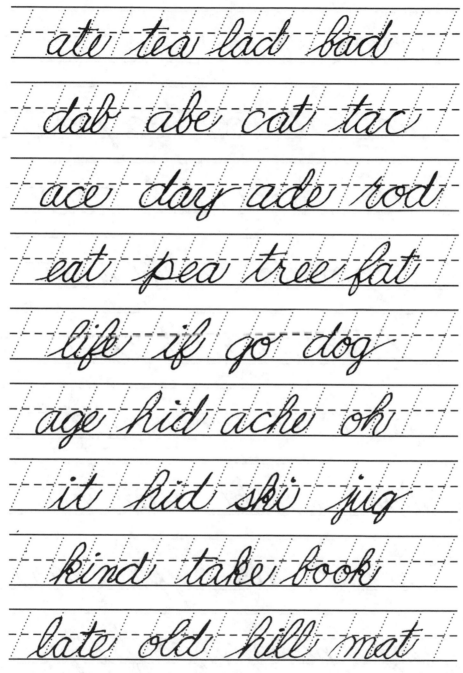

ate tea lad bad

dab abe cat tac

ace day ade rod

eat pea tree fat

life if go dog

age hid ache oh

it hid ski jug

kind take book

late old hill mat

(continues)

Cursive Practice Sample (continued)

come aim no end

an oat toe too pad

ape loop rail air

arm star ask lass

tag art ate use

put out you vat

give with own new

x-ray next fix year

eye many zoo fuzz

Cursive Practice Paper

ADDITION TABLE

+	1	2	3	4	5	6	7	8	9
1									
2									
3									
4									
5									
6									
7									
8									
9									

MULTIPLICATION TABLE

X	1	2	3	4	5	6	7	8	9
1									
2									
3									
4									
5									
6									
7									
8									
9									

✓ Special Project Checklist

STEP   **DATE DONE**

☐ **1.** Decide on a project theme.   _____

☐ **2.** Have theme approved by teacher.   _____

THEME: _____

☐ **3.** Make a list of the things that need to be done and the order in which they should be completed. (List, then number each task.)

☐ **4.** Decide who is going to do what. (Initial each task.)

☐ **5.** Set deadlines for completion of each task. (Write in the dates.)

TASK	DATE DUE	DATE DONE	PERSON RESPONSIBLE

☐ **6.** Make a list of materials needed.

(continues)

✓ Special Project Checklist (continued)

☐ **7.** Make a projected budget. (Write the estimated cost of each item.)

TASK   **COST**

_____ _____

_____ _____

_____ _____

_____ _____

☐ **8.** Send away for resource materials needed.

RESOURCE MATERIAL   **DATE REQUESTED**   **DATE RECEIVED**

_____ _____ _____

_____ _____ _____

_____ _____ _____

☐ **9.** Contact community resources.

COMMUNITY RESOURCE   **DATE CONTACTED**

_____ _____

_____ _____

_____ _____

☐ **10.** Visit the library and do research on the Internet.

PURPOSE OF VISIT   **DATE OF VISIT**

_____ _____

_____ _____

_____ _____

☐ **11.** Complete the project on schedule.

DATE TURNED IN: _____   **GRADE:** _____

 # SPECIAL PROJECT AGREEMENT FORM

TODAY'S DATE: _____   **DUE DATE:** _____

PROJECT THEME: _____

I, _____ , agree to do the following tasks by myself. I agree to do them on time.
     STUDENT'S NAME

TASK	DATE DUE

I, _____ , and I, _____ , agree to do the following
    PARENT'S NAME   STUDENT'S NAME

tasks together. We agree to do them on time.

TASK	DATE DUE

BOOK REPORT OUTLINE

I. INTRODUCTION

A. Title of book: _____

B. Author: _____

C. Type of book (*example:* mystery, adventure, fantasy):

_____

D. Setting of book

Time: _____

Place: _____

E. Why I read this book: _____

_____

II. MAIN CHARACTERS

_____

_____

_____

_____

_____

_____

_____ **(CONTINUES)**

III. SUMMARY OF BOOK

_____

_____

_____

_____

_____

IV. MY FEELINGS ABOUT THIS BOOK

A. The part I liked best: _____

_____

_____

B. The part I liked least: _____

_____

_____

C. This book was (check one)

☐ hard to read   ☐ easy to read   ☐ in between

D. I (check one)

☐ would   ☐ would not

recommend this book to someone else because: _____

_____

_____

BOOK REPORT OUTLINE

I. INTRODUCTION

A. Title of book: _____

B. Author: _____

C. Type of book (*example:* mystery, adventure, fantasy):

_____

D. Setting of book

Time: _____

Place: _____

E. Why I read this book: _____

_____

II. CHARACTERS

A. Main character (name and description): _____

_____

_____

B. Other important characters (names and descriptions): _____

_____

_____

(CONTINUES)

III. SUMMARY OF PLOT

_____

_____

_____

_____

IV. CRITIQUE

A. The part I liked best: _____

_____

_____

B. The part I liked least: _____

_____

_____

C. This book was (check one)

☐ hard to read   ☐ easy to read   ☐ in between

D. I (check one)

☐ would   ☐ would not

recommend this book to someone else because: _____

_____

_____

NONFICTION
BOOK REPORT OUTLINE

I. INTRODUCTION

A. Title of book: _____

B. Author: _____

C. Subject of book: _____

_____

D. Why I read this book: _____

_____

_____

II. SUMMARY OF BOOK

_____

_____

_____

_____

_____

_____

_____

_____

(CONTINUES)

III. NEW AND INTERESTING FACTS I LEARNED FROM READING THIS BOOK

_____

_____

_____

_____

IV. MY FEELINGS ABOUT THIS BOOK

A. The part I liked best: _____

_____

_____

B. The part I liked least: _____

_____

_____

C. This book was (check one)

☐ hard to read   ☐ easy to read   ☐ in between

D. I (check one)

☐ would   ☐ would not

recommend this book to someone else because: _____

_____

_____

NONFICTION
BOOK REPORT OUTLINE

I. Introduction

   A. Title of book: _____

   B. Author: _____

   C. Subject of book: _____

   _____

II. Summary of book

_____

_____

_____

_____

_____

_____

_____

_____

_____

_____

_____ (CONTINUES)

III. New and interesting facts I learned from reading this book

_____

_____

_____

_____

IV. Critique

A. The part I liked best: _____

_____

_____

B. The part I liked least: _____

_____

_____

C. This book was (check one)

☐ hard to read   ☐ easy to read   ☐ in between

D. I (check one)

☐ would   ☐ would not

recommend this book to someone else because: _____

_____

_____

BIOGRAPHY
BOOK REPORT OUTLINE

I. INTRODUCTION

A. Title of book: _____

B. Author: _____

C. Who the book was about: _____

D. Why I read this book: _____

_____

II. WHAT I LEARNED ABOUT THIS PERSON

_____

_____

_____

_____

_____

_____

_____

_____

_____

_____ **(CONTINUES)**

BIOGRAPHY BOOK REPORT OUTLINE (CONTINUED)

III. WHY THIS PERSON IS REMEMBERED OR ADMIRED TODAY

_____

_____

_____

_____

IV. MY FEELING ABOUT THIS BOOK

A. The part I liked best: _____

_____

_____

B. The part I liked least: _____

_____

_____

C. This book was (check one)

☐ hard to read   ☐ easy to read   ☐ in between

D. I (check one)

☐ would   ☐ would not

recommend this book to someone else because: _____

_____

_____

BIOGRAPHY
BOOK REPORT OUTLINE

I. INTRODUCTION

   A. Title of book: _____

   B. Author: _____

   C. Who the book was about: _____

   D. Why I read this book: _____

   _____

II. SUMMARY OF BOOK

   A. What I learned about the person's life: _____

   _____

   _____

   _____

   B. What I learned about the person's major achievements:

   _____

   _____

   _____

   _____ (CONTINUES)

BIOGRAPHY BOOK REPORT OUTLINE (CONTINUED)

III. PROBLEMS

A. The major problem in the person's life was: _____

_____

B. Here is how this problem was solved: _____

_____

IV. WHY THIS PERSON IS REMEMBERED OR ADMIRED TODAY

_____

V. CRITIQUE

A. The part I liked best: _____

_____

_____

B. The part I liked least: _____

_____

_____

C. This book was (check one)

☐ hard to read　　☐ easy to read　　☐ in between

D. I (check one)

☐ would　　☐ would not

recommend this book to someone else because: _____

_____

# Term Paper Checklist

ASSIGNMENT: To write a term paper on: _____

_____

DATE DUE: _____

REQUIREMENTS:

My paper will need

☐ a title page

☐ a table of contents

☐ a bibliography

☐ graphics

    What kinds of graphics? _____

_____

It should be   ☐ handwritten   ☐ typed

STEP	DATE DUE	DATE DONE
☐ 1. Choose a topic	_____	_____
☐ 2. Have topic approved by teacher	_____	_____
☐ 3. Do library and Internet research	_____	_____
☐ 4. Contact community resources for information		

NAME OF RESOURCE	DATE DUE	DATE DONE
_____	_____	_____
_____	_____	_____
_____	_____	_____

(continues)

✔ Term Paper Checklist (continued)

☐ 5. Write letters to obtain information from national sources

WROTE LETTERS TO	DATE DUE	DATE DONE

☐ 6. Take notes

TOOK NOTES FROM THESE SOURCES

☐ 7. Do an outline

☐ 8. Write a rough draft

☐ 9. Proofread rough draft; make corrections

☐ 10. Write final draft

☐ 11. Turn final draft in to teacher

BINGO GAME CARDS

B	I	N	G	O
1				
2				
3				
4				
5				

B	I	N	G	O
1				
2				
3				
4				
5				

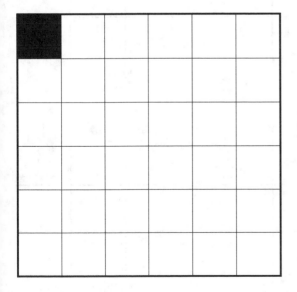

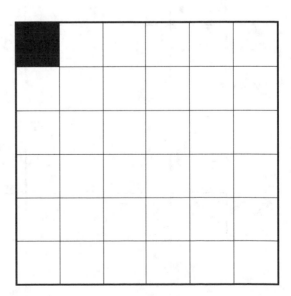

TIC-TAC-TOE BOARDS

DOTS GAME BOARDS

Index

About the Author

 Jeanne Shay Schumm, Ph.D., is a professor and chair of the Department of Teaching and Learning at the University of Miami School of Education. She teaches courses in reading assessment and instruction and is actively engaged in research on reading. In addition to coauthoring over 75 research articles, Jeanne is the author of *School Power: Study Skill Strategies for Succeeding in School* (Free Spirit Publishing, 2001) and is coauthor of *The Reading Tutor's Handbook: A Commonsense Guide to Helping Students Read and Write* (Free Spirit Publishing, 1999) with her husband, Gerald E. Schumm Jr., D. Min. Jeanne enjoys helping her grandson, Jack DeFraites (who lives in New Orleans with his mom, Jamie, and dad, John) with his home learning.

Other Great Books from Free Spirit

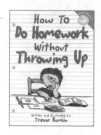

How to Do Homework Without Throwing Up
written and illustrated by Trevor Romain
This book features hilarious cartoons and witty insights that teach important truths about homework and positive, practical strategies for getting it done. For ages 8–13.
$8.95; 72 pp.; softcover; illus.; 5⅛" x 7"

True or False? Tests Stink!
by Trevor Romain and Elizabeth Verdick
This book offers proven strategies and practical advice...plus plenty of humor and goofy cartoons. Kids will smile and laugh as they discover tips and information that will help them survive and thrive in all kinds of test situations. For ages 8–13.
$9.95; 88 pp.; softcover; illus.; 5⅛" x 7"

School Power
Study Skill Strategies for Succeeding in School
Revised and Updated Edition
by Jeanne Shay Schumm, Ph.D.
This popular study-skills handbook, newly revised and updated, covers everything students need to know, including how to get organized, take notes, do Internet research, write better, read faster, study smarter, handle long-term assignments, and more. For ages 11 & up.
$16.95; 144 pp.; softcover; illus.; 8½" x 11"

To place an order or to request a free catalog of SELF-HELP FOR KIDS® and SELF-HELP FOR TEENS® materials, please write, call, email, or visit our Web site:

Free Spirit Publishing Inc.
217 Fifth Avenue North • Suite 200 • Minneapolis, MN 55401-1299
toll-free 800.735.7323 • local 612.338.2068 • fax 612.337.5050
help4kids@freespirit.com • www.freespirit.com